Arthur Darack formerly wrote the
nationally syndicated news column
"Buy Right" and heads Consumer
Group, Inc., a publishing and research
company. He is the author of *Consumer
Digest's Auto Buyer's Guide, 1976;
Repair Your Car*; and *The Playboy
Book of Sports Car Maintenance and
Repair*, and is a contributing editor to
"The Moneyletter."

Arthur Darack
and the
staff of Consumer Group, Inc.

USED CARS
How to Avoid Highway Robbery

Prentice-Hall, Inc., Englewood Cliffs, New Jersey 07632

Library of Congress Cataloging in Publication Data

Darack, Arthur.
　Used cars.

　Includes index.
　1.　Used cars—Purchasing.　I.　Title.
TL162.D37　　1983　　629.2'222　　82-13161
ISBN 0-13-940056-7
ISBN 0-13-940049-4 (A Reward book : pbk.)

This book is available at a special discount when ordered in
bulk quantities. Contact Prentice-Hall, Inc., General
Publishing Division, Special Sales, Englewood Cliffs, New Jersey 07632.

1　　2　　3　　4　　5　　6　　7　　8　　9　　10

ISBN 0-13-940056-7

ISBN 0-13-940049-4 {PBK.}

Editorial/production supervision by Chris McMorrow
Cover design by Hal Siegel
Cover illustration by Jim Kinstrey
Manufacturing buyer: Edmund W. Leone

Prentice-Hall International, Inc., *London*
Prentice-Hall of Australia Pty. Limited, *Sydney*
Prentice-Hall Canada Inc., *Toronto*
Prentice-Hall of India Private Limited, *New Delhi*
Prentice-Hall of Japan, Inc., *Tokyo*
Prentice-Hall of Southeast Asia Pte. Ltd., *Singapore*
Whitehall Books Limited, *Wellington, New Zealand*
Editora Prentice-Hall do Brasil Ltda., *Rio de Janeiro*

Contents

15. Foreign Car Prices/196

Preface

The word *lemon* plays as central a role in used-car parlance and consciousness as it does in citrus fruit. A sour category of new and used cars is denoted that indicates terminal illness or worse. Is there such a thing, or is it imagination?

There are plenty of badly designed systems out there in all nationalities of cars. U.S. cars do not have a monopoly on them. To a mechanic a system is a lemon if it is difficult to fix—almost every electrical system, for example. Cooling systems on all cars are "lemons" in the sense that they self-destruct over time. But so do all systems. Some cars do have systems that are badly designed from the standpoint that they aren't reliable. The old Corvair's fan belt system is an example, and many years ago Buick put out an engine with a radiator that lacked adequate cooling capacity. Many cars are underpowered, and in the old days virtually all cars were overpowered.

Safety systems such as steering and braking are more or less foolproof, though it wasn't always that way. Until the advent of the dual diagonal brake systems, in which one system will stop the car if the other fails, brakes were a weak, dangerous link. Steering systems are either ball recirculating systems or rack and pinion. They are standardized and they present difficulty only when what they are attached to—wheels and links—deteriorate. There was a claim by *Consumer Reports* magazine in 1978 that the Dodge Omni–Plymouth Horizon power steering system was defective, but it was a standard system as good—that is, as reliable—as any other and better than most, as subsequent tests and sales proved.

But are there no lemons? That is, cars that cannot be made to perform acceptably? Probably not. In early Subaru models the front brakes were very difficult to repair and tricky to adjust, but you could do both if you knew how and put in the time and effort. Some Holley carburetors are tricky, but all carburetors require great care in overhauling, and anyone who can fix an old Carter can do the same deed on a new Holley. Weber carburetors by Holley are even trickier. The VW Rabbit has a number of systems that veer toward the category of the lemon, but all can be repaired. The earliest models (1975) were the big culprits, and recently most problems have been cleared up. Not only did they have wear-prone valve guides but also fuse boxes that self-destructed when rained on—a common occurrence, thanks to a badly designed fender grommet that allowed water to pass through with the radio antenna. But you could throw a cover over the box, if you knew about it, or even fix the grommet.

Every MacPherson strut is a lemon in the sense that it is much more difficult to fix than any earlier linked system of front suspension, because much more disassembly is required. But viewed in terms of performance, it's a simpler system, therefore better, than the one it replaces. Nowadays, virtually all front-drive cars have the strut system.

Strut systems are not weak links. These wretched "lemon-flavored" devices are found elsewhere—in cooling and ignition, starting and cranking, and other electrical areas. Fuel systems also veer toward the soured state, especially since the advent of emission controls. Electronic ignition systems are among the worst offenders because they are not supposed to fail, but they do, and when they do—without warning, usually—they can strand you, unlike the mechanical systems they replaced. But fan belts can also strand you, and except in the old Corvair, they are not in the class of unreliable components. They simply wear out and if replaced regularly will never cause trouble.

So we have come full circle. Are there, then, no lemons? Only among individual systems, I would say. I do not count such things as rust-prone areas in bodies, which are found in many if not most cars, or such things as windows that won't go up and down easily or dome lights that can't be repaired. These are annoyances but not fatal defects. Every system can be a lemon; every system can perform as desired. What converts the one into the other is ordinary wear, premature wear due to metal fatigue or carelessness of the operator, or some miscalculation of design. The great recalls of recent years offer proof that plenty of designs have not been perfect. The flap over the Ford automatic transmission that slipped out of "Park" and into "Reverse" is a case in point in that it combined some miscalculation of design and some driver carelessness. Ford said it was all driver carelessness; the Department of Transportation and Ralph Nader said more or less the opposite. It was different in that it required one extra motion from the operator that other transmissions did not. If you were born and raised with a General Motors automatic transmission, you would agree with DOT and Nader; if with a Ford transmission, you might agree with Ford.

Is there no reason to choose one car over another?

Many publications claim you should buy this car, not that.

Every salesman makes the same claim. We will examine these and similar claims in detail.

I wish to expess my appreciation to the following companies for providing the illustrative material used in this book: *American Motors Corp.; Cadillac Motor Division, GM Corp.; Chevrolet Motor Division, GM Corp.; Chrysler-Plymouth; Fiat*

Motors of North America, Inc.; Ford Motor Corp.; Mazda Motors of America, Inc.; Mercedes-Benz of North America; Nissan Motor Co.; Oldsmobile Division, GM Corp.; Pontiac Motor Division, GM Corp.; Renault USA; Subaru of America, Inc.; Toyota Motor Sales USA; and *VW of America, Inc.*

Used Cars

Introduction

Selling used cars is viewed in many quarters as a dishonest, reprehensible activity, one step removed from felony, and it is not clear whether the step is above or below. So it comes as no surprise to learn that much of what is written about buying used cars is in a class with that low view of the activity itself. *Consumer Reports* magazine, our most prestigious journal devoted to sorting out what you ought to buy in the marketplace, has established charts of automobile frequency of repair that purport to sort out lemons from bargains. These charts do one thing instantly: They make it clear that U.S. cars are inferior to imports. The charts announce at a glance that anyone who buys a used hunk of Detroit iron is a fool or worse.

Here is the way they "work." The magazine mails cards to subscribers inviting them to participate in the rating of cars. Several hundred thousand of their roughly two million subscribers respond, checking boxes to indicate what kind of performance they've had with their car's basic systems. What results is an indictment of U.S. cars.

1

Yet the responses do not provide two key pieces of information without which the charts are worse than meaningless: (1) the type of driver who is responding (careful, scrupulous as to maintenance, and so on) and (2) the mileage of the system in question when it broke down. All car systems of whatever nationality have a life expectancy. Sometimes it varies between similar components—say, a starting motor in a Chevrolet Vega or a VW Rabbit. Here, life expectancy favors the Rabbit. It isn't always that way with General Motors starters, which are made by Delco. It's usually the other way around; moreover, Delco makes starters for cars all over the world. The auto parts industry is international. But if the driver uses the starter two or three times as often because he doesn't have the engine tuned at prescribed intervals so as to permit rapid starting, he will condemn the starter to early death. The Vega was a touchy, even tragic car. It was designed to combat the imports. It has a four-cylinder engine wedded to the usual Detroit front engine–rear-drive scheme. But if you bought it with a stick shift and resisted air conditioning, it was a good gas mileage car (16 or 17 city; 30 or more country). Beginning with the 1975 model, it had the new General Motors electronic ignition system with fairly advanced fuel system. The engine had an aluminum block (shades of the Corvair). It was a shy innovator.

But the fuel and ignition systems were touchy, and aluminum simply doesn't wear as well as cast iron in auto engines. Valve guides often wore out, although not as early as in a typical 1975 VW Rabbit, many of which needed valve jobs between 30,000 and 40,000 miles. The carburetion system, with its advanced Holley carburetor and special solenoid choke, was too clever for its own good: The choke wouldn't close to permit starting, and nobody could figure out why not. Despite all that, the Vega, beginning in 1975, when its rust problems were minimized, was an enormously appealing car. However, *Consumer Reports* magazine declared that it was a disaster and nobody should buy such an automobile. Exit Vega soon thereafter, justifiably or not, and I would say not.

General Motors could survive the loss of the Vega, as it

had the Corvair. Again, General Motors was blamed for an innovative car (though not in a class with Corvair). People will not accept blame if they can blame General Motors. Why doesn't this happen with imports?

For one thing, until very recently, imports were only a small percentage of the cars reported on in *Consumer Reports* charts of frequency of repair. They reflected the newness of the mass introduction of foreign cars into the U.S. market. Typically, people bought them for better gas mileage and better durability and performance. So they had an emotional investment with respect to their judgment, of a sort that most U.S. car buyers wouldn't necessarily have. Also, if the imports couldn't gain wide acceptance, there was the possibility of a bad investment and you could lose your money, or part of it. If a little cheerleading could help in the protection of your investment, who would know? It's the sensible thing to do for any educated consumer. So the imports have to be better.

In effect, the frequency-of-repair charts were pitting about 85 percent or more of the cars against about 15 percent, and the 15 percent reflected special reasons for revealing or concealing information. Also, it is not information that most people will keep with accuracy. You would have to maintain data constantly—a bookkeeping chore. In these days of the multiplication of records, few people will make such an effort. Finally, the two keys—mileage and type of driver—were not even solicited by *Consumer Reports*, and without that information the charts are misleading.

Meanwhile, the media reported with glowing approval the "inside" information—the suppressed truth, if you will—about the auto products of corporate America.

These *Consumer Reports* charts even lack internal consistency. For the past several years the magazine has warned people away from various Subaru models, yet their own frequency-of-repair charts showed Subaru to be one of the cars least prone to frequent repairs and also one of the best mileage cars. Nor did they have anything drastically negative to discover about other aspects—drivability. Beginning in 1969 and 1970, when Subaru introduced its four-cylinder, high-

FIGURE 1. A Subaru station wagon, 1978 model. For low-cost transportation, this front-wheel-drive car is hard to beat, when bought at the right price.

mileage car, the Subaru has had growing market acceptance. There are indeed many objective grounds for praising the car. Its opposed four-cylinder engine was extraordinarily effective in developing its power to the maximum, and it had an extremely innovative cooling system (two radiators, instead of one, and not pressurized so that it enjoyed much greater life expectancy than all other cooling systems) and, in early models, an interesting suspension system (which, alas, was abandoned for more conventional components and design, probably because of *Consumer Reports* criticism). More recently, Subaru has been highly innovative with its extra combustion process that lowers emissions—a stratified charge concept. Subaru's front-drive power system has always been durable and excellent, though other gearboxes surpass it in smoothness and ease (Chrysler's Omni, for example). None of these facts and features were reflected in the *Consumer Reports* frequency-of-repair charts other than it was a much better than average car. Despite that, the magazine warned people against buying the car until recent models came out. These models, as indicated, are better in some ways, inferior in others. On balance, the car

4

remains a highly desirable product and always was (except for a model brought over in the late 1960s, which was the equivalent of a motorcycle with a box over it). Yet the magazine constantly touted other imports far above Subaru while its frequency-of-repair charts urged the buying of that car by implication. In many cases, media reporters, anxious to discredit U.S. corporations, do not report such matters as these. They are too technical, too dry and lacking in shock value.

Does it follow that no objective criteria exist for the buyer of a used car? Nothing of the sort. Criteria do indeed exist and will be argued in the chapters to follow, but they are not questions of polling or voting; they are largely mechanical questions having to do with mileage and condition and, in a few cases, with questions of design. Admittedly, there is much subjectivity in these matters. For example, a car such as the recent MGB would be condemned by many people because of the closeness of brake and accelerator and the possibility of tramping on the gas when you want to brake. Yet a little practice will guide you to the right control and sports car lovers—mostly young people—are used to the kind of finicky distinction involved.

There are less subjective matters. I noted the Vega's problems and, having defended that car, I should note that aluminum engines do not wear as well as engines with cast iron blocks. Practically that means an early engine overhaul, which most people would consider an insuperable objection to that car. But engine overhauls are not that expensive or difficult, if you can buy the car at the right price. So I would suggest, contrary to the verdict of *Consumer Reports* magazine, that the Vega is indeed a buyable used car, but it should be bought at a heavy discount in the almost certain knowledge that an engine overhaul will be needed. Yet many small cars fall into that category, and they aren't singled out by this or that authority. Any four-cylinder engine works twice as hard as any eight. So they don't last as long. People used to driving typical Detroit products for the past thirty years will be appalled to learn that engines half the size don't last as long. That's not an invariable formula. If you take care of a four-cylinder engine, you can expect about 100,000 miles on a set of valves, rings, bearings, and other basic components that require replacement in an overhaul. And taking care isn't that much more than a regular oil change, as well as changing the filters in the air and fuel systems and keeping all liquids at specified levels. Not many people are willing to be so conscientious because conscience in these matters is costly. That brings us to the next discussion—the reduction of costs.

If you learn to do these elementary maintenance procedures to a car, you can lower costs sharply and prolong the life of the car enormously. If you go one step beyond and learn to repair the car, you can bring down the cost of running it by about a third. In the process, you will acquire a basic knowledge of cars that will enable you to buy used cars instead of new, obtaining roughly equivalent performance without paying huge depreciation costs.

These are the kinds of objective criteria that mean most to a used-car buyer—the systems and their condition, and costs. It goes without saying that you ought to buy a car you like.

HOW TO USE THIS BOOK

The book is divided into three main parts.

Part I explains the breakdown systems in cars, the nature of their defects, how to identify them, and the costs to repair them. Many individual car makes and models enter into this discussion. Part II analyzes the car markets, focusing at first on general considerations, then on discussions of world car markets, manufacturers, and products. Part III gives buying advice, with makes and models from 1975 forward, sometimes talking about earlier models when appropriate. Statistical material includes prices, weights, sizes, mileages, and other data. Buying recommendations are a frequent feature, with many comparisons.

I
THE BREAKDOWN SYSTEMS

1

General Considerations

USED CAR MYTHS

I suggest that one key myth is that of the "lemon," the car that should only be junked because of its endless chain of repairs. Few such cars exist, if you allow for the fact that all systems do wear out sooner or later—some much sooner than later. You can repair every system if you are willing to make the investment. If an engine doesn't perform to your satisfaction, you can have it overhauled or replaced; the same applies to every other system. But that's expensive, unless you are a home mechanic and pay only for the parts. Usually such radical replacements are unnecessary. To cite a common complaint, when a fuel system breaks down, it usually begins with the carburetor or fuel pump. Cleaning out the carburetor and replacing such parts as the needle valve assembly and the various small links in the pumping chain will restore performance. Fuel pumps cost about $20, less in some cases. You can replace it yourself rather easily, or you can have it done with

FIGURE 2. This large four-barrel carburetor is found on many V-8 engines of the middle and late 1970s models. It is used throughout GM lines.

the understanding that the garage must be paid for its labors and the housing of parts. Translated, that means if you have someone else do the work, you pay from three to five times what it costs when you supply the labor and buy the part yourself at a discount.

Other common system complaints are comparably handled. However, some cars are so worn out because of mileage—especially abused mileage—that they are not worth repairing. That is another story. If the car has been driven by a determined "hot rodder" and has not been oiled and greased regularly at specified intervals, it might have fatal deterioration in too many systems to make salvage worthwhile. But such cars are not as common as the lemon myth makes it out. Every used car has something wrong with it, and it is vital that you know what the defects are. That is the point of this book: to teach you about such defects. Dealers and other sellers are under no legal obligation to give you that information—if, indeed, they have it. Also, catastrophic defects—the kind that show up on the expressway and strand you—often betray few if any warning symptoms.

Body rust, if severe, is the one exception to the theory that the lemon myth is an exaggeration. Body rust can be sufficiently advanced to disqualify any used car—again, unless you are a home mechanic willing to do the radical surgery that most body shops wouldn't touch, or if they would, the "touch" on your wallet would be too severe to accept. Thus, there are two classes of used cars: those you should consider only if you can repair them and all the others. Since most people are not in the auto repair business nor have any intention of entering it, our discussions will concentrate on recognizing what to avoid.

Does that automatically eliminate certain makes and models? We have already discussed in the Introduction *Consumer Reports* magazine's earnest attempts to systematize used-car buying by make and model. We have rejected it on the grounds that the field is too complex to be reduced to such formulas, despite the best intentions. Still, there are some general approaches. One can admit that in the U.S. it is probably best to avoid Pinto and Vega—Vega because of the aluminum block engine, which simply doesn't wear as well as cast iron, and Pinto because of the bad news that accompanied it, whether deserved or not.

What about untouchable imports? Perhaps the Mazda rotary qualifies. Its engine seals broke down in an alarming percentage of cases, making a costly overhaul mandatory. Also, the rotary engine didn't quite cut the gas mileage mustard as it was supposed to; mileages never got enough over 20 miles per gallon to warrant using its engine rather than the horde of economical engines that appeared.

If you are a disciple of the "contrary opinion" school (best known in stock market analysis), you will now rush out and look for used Vegas, Pintos, and Mazdas exclusively. You could be right. These cars often sell below comparable used cars, and you could get one that defies the odds—which aren't that great against them. Beginning in 1975, for example,

Vega's rust symptoms that plagued earlier models were over-come. And no matter how much wear the engines might suffer, every engine *can* be repaired. Similar arguments might be made on behalf of Mazda and Pinto, though you deal mostly with bad news in the case of Pinto, which isn't easily dis-counted.

Fashions in used cars are unpredictable. Big cars, small cars, medium-size cars—all pop in and out of the bestseller list. Imports have grown inexorably, based mostly on their better gas mileages. Also, Japanese cars have one enormous price advantage based on much lower labor-production costs, so that many small Japanese cars sell below U.S. and Euro-pean small cars. Further, imports—both Japanese and European—have an aura of quality that often surpasses the perception U.S. buyers have of the native beast. So, the imports have surged to almost a third of the U.S. car market. That market penetration also includes, of course, the ex-pensive group: Mercedes, BMW, Saab, Volvo, Jaguar, Rolls Royce, and so forth. These cars, reputed to be far better than U.S. cars, mostly have no counterparts in the U.S. market, and their aura undoubtedly wore off on the lower-priced, gas-sipping models to some extent. High-priced U.S. cars don't have the kind of posh, above-it-all image possessed by the Mercedes, Rolls, Lamborghini brigade. People actually believed that these expensive imports didn't have the breakdown sys-tems of their Chevies and Plymouths. Alas, for the U.S. market, both high- and low-priced, everything seemed to favor the imports when the Arab oil embargo struck in 1973 and there were no small U.S. cars except Vega and Pinto. Since 1973 the U.S. auto makers have been trying desperately to catch up. It is not an easy game.

Prior to World War II, imports were primarily such ex-pensive models as Rolls, Jaguar, and others. VW was the first successful low-priced car, ironically from Germany, the coun-try we had defeated. France and Italy entered the import derby, but VW won. Its rear-engine "bug" made enormous sales inroads, thanks to Detroit's failure to enter the market. Its "ugly duckling" design, with an economical engine that had no counterpart in the U.S., gave it a reputation for thrift, ingenuity, and durability. These qualities wore off on the reputation of later VWs, including Rabbit, Dasher, the related Audi, and others. VW became an enduring symbol of qualities in cars Detroit wasn't producing that many Americans wanted. After the oil embargo virtually all Americans wanted them.

Japanese cars, which trickled over in the 1960s, turned into the flood we now know, thanks in part to the price-competitive factor (also to the favorable rate of exchange), and thanks also to the carefully orchestrated reputation for quality the cars came to enjoy. High quality and low cost are incomparable sales lubricants, given an absorbing market. One other factor entered to grease the imports' path: the native U.S. consumer movement, which had as one of its chief articles of faith the inferiority of the U.S. product. It didn't matter that many of the early Japanese cars were crude copies of U.S. models, or that many of the Japanese systems were almost ridiculously complicated, prone to failure, and costly to repair. Japanese cars *had* to be better, as the consumer faith saw it, because they came from those shrines of industrial purity erected by Nissan and Toyota for the purpose of teaching the world how to ride economically rather than ostentatiously. But anyone tackling a brake job on an early Subaru, with the brakes hugging the engine, would more likely utter an ancient Shōgun curse at so terrible a design. (The system was later modified.)

Japanese and German cars came to be prized above all others. It must be admitted that some of this veneration is deserved. The new Rabbit, once it got all the bugs (no pun intended) out of its system, is a great car. But the several purification rites attendant on the ridding of the bugs caused untold agonies for U.S. buyers. Price hikes also took their toll. Now you can buy U.S. cars by Chrysler that started out as carbon copies of the Rabbit—with several key Chrysler modifications that sometimes improved the designs—for less than the VW originals. And the typical Toyota and Datsun cars at the low-priced end of the spectrum, with front engine–rear drive, could hardly be told from the stick-in-the-mud Chevette.

But myths die harder than the realities (if any) behind them, and the fact remains that small imports on the used-car lots sell more rapidly than any other models, and when the imports speak Japanese, they go most rapidly of all.

Increasingly this makes little sense, in view of the Chrysler front-drive copies of VW, the innovative General Motors X-Cars, the newer J-Cars, and Ford's Escort. Soon Detroit will have a wider, more varied repertory to compete with Japan and Europe, even without the battery of sporty makes and models available from overseas. But the sporty scene will be made by Detroit in time, since a trickle is now beginning.

That will leave only the top group of expensive, luxury cars for Detroit to explore. Mercedes, Rolls, Lamborghini, and so on seem fairly secure as of this writing. Detroit's answer to that group, so far, is to gussy up standard luxury models and raise prices astronomically. This tactic hasn't worked and won't. What that means, for the used-car buyer, is that the prices of the luxury imports will remain high. A cottage industry of restoration exists in these cars around the country. The amount of restoration determines the price.

One vexing aspect of foreign cars is their repair. Parts cost more; the typical U.S. mechanic is unfamiliar with them (though that is changing rapidly), and it is easy to pay twice as much for familiar jobs. Anyone about to buy a first foreign car should be aware of such matters. The salesman will not rush to volunteer it.

This brief overview of used-car history is offered as an orientation for the used-car buyer. One should know that the car industry is becoming more internationalized than ever, and even General Motors cars now sport features once available only on imports—MacPherson struts, for example. As cars become more internationalized, the buyer won't be able to take refuge in a particular make or model in order to escape undesirable systems. For example, many people continue to yearn for mechanical ignition in order to escape the detested electronic systems that strand you without warning (a desertion no mechanical system would countenance). The melancholy fact is that few mechanical systems remain, and fewer can be expected in the future. If that's not bad enough, electronic fuel injection systems will proliferate as well, dooming that system to the computer and its whims. Once you put a computer on board—which you do with electronic ignition—there is no limit to what the devil can do. It's like the impact on bachelorhood described by Henry Higgins in *My Fair Lady*, who sang woefully about the effects of "letting a woman" into his life. To be sure, some fail-safe compensations are being designed into computerized ignition and fuel systems, but it will take another decade or so to produce a truly safe system—one roughly comparable with the mechanical systems of long ago which gave ample warning of failure. This is not to say that mechanical systems don't also strand you; they certainly do. We'll note these matters as we go along, since some systems are more likely to wear out within certain mileages than others. Moreover, test-driving will not reveal all of them.

TEST-DRIVING

Test-driving is important if you know what to look for, and you should not buy a used car (or a new one, for that matter) without driving it.

Test-driving, if accompanied by a careful look at the engine, before and afterward, can be the difference between a good and bad car in your life. Let's begin with the obvious things first.

Climate is important. If you live in a northern area with cold winters, make sure the car starts readily. In other words, start the car yourself in the coldest possible weather, but not after someone else has started it recently. How can you tell that? Not easily, if the salesman won't be honest about it. Also, it's hard to test air conditioning in the dead of winter. The air is bound to come out the same temperature as the weather if the compressor isn't working. In summer you merely turn it on; it cools or it doesn't.

But starting is a vital key to performance. If the car won't start quickly and flawlessly, and idle quietly and steadily, it means trouble. It could mean minor trouble—merely a carburetor adjustment—or it could mean major trouble, from big engine work to ignition and fuel system overhaul. Modern electronic ignition systems are expensive to overhaul, and so are fuel systems, especially electronic and other fuel injection systems. So be wary of a car that starts with difficulty and doesn't idle fluently. Yet these are key reasons people get rid of cars.

There are many reasons to test-drive, including the enhancement of your knowledge about various cars. You can't make a career out of driving used cars, but unless you know the feel of good brakes as well as how they work, how various stick shifts perform well or badly, and so on, you won't be a very wise buyer. All the books in the world won't help if you've never heard telltale motor noises, stepped on brakes that squeak or shudder, used steering systems that wobble, and so on. Merely because you've been driving for years, even with a variety of cars, doesn't necessarily qualify you to make the necessary distinctions. Your cars may have accustomed you to bad brakes, poor steering, or your cars may have been without vital defects. It can happen. In some ways the best car I ever had was a 1960 Chevrolet; only I was too inexperienced to know it at the time. The reason it was the best was that it arrived at the age of 96,000 miles virtually flawless, allowing for normal replacements—which I made or bought. In my ignorance I thought all cars did that. They don't. Was the 1960 Chevrolet the best car ever made? Undoubtedly not, but it had typical Chevrolet engineering of the period, aimed at durability and convenience. GM and other manufacturers continue to aim for these things. Their job is tougher.

I've stressed the need to examine engines carefully. Professional test drivers make much of access for repairs, complaining when an oil filter isn't sticking out at them, or spark plugs don't smile when touched. Don't be put off by such talk. Ease of access to one part will be canceled out by another that is hard to reach.

The test-driving of cars has brought a new vocabulary out of the woodwork. Terms such as *over-steer, under-steer, road feel, cornering,* and so on, are used. What do they mean?

Essentially nothing; they are for professional drivers who have conjured up a terminology to cloak the fact that what they do is irrelevant to what you want in a car. All you need to know about the things they test—steering, braking, parking, seeing (visibility), mileage, convenience, comfort, starting, accessories, road handling, and suspension style—can be stated and understood in plain English. Most are subjective. The national flap started by *Consumer Reports* magazine over the Omni steering when the car first appeared is an example. A test driver didn't like it; that's what it came down to, based on his test that he could make it do terrible things more easily than he could with some other car or cars. If your norm is to do terrible things in a car, such tests may be of interest. But if you drive as intended, safely and to get somewhere in comfort, sharing the road at all times, you will find Omni steering as good as any on the road. Steering and all the other activities of car driving are so standardized that the tiny differences from car to car admit to quick and easy familiarity. Only professional drivers can detect differences, which they magnify. If you are in an occult profession, it is important to you that you make significant discoveries in it—like turning up a manuscript showing a fingering used by J. S. Bach. This could cause a rash of musicology, promotions, and careers. We have already discussed all the important things about braking, ridability, comfort, and so on. They are all mechanical, involving systems and designs. Test drivers do not concern themselves with such mundane matters.

So when you test-drive a used car, you will automatically compare it with the car you drove most often. Comparisons are inevitable and can be helpful. If the steering differs very much from your car, you must ask yourself the questions that involve both your reactions and your feelings. If you think your reaction times will be very different, you might think twice about the car, especially if you feel that you don't like it. The same assessments are in order with braking, accelerating, shifting, using the controls and the convenience and luxury items. Try them all for (1) reaction times and (2) feelings about them. Don't worry about what experts say.

CAR SAFETY

Cars not only frustrate; they also kill. Studies by government and private groups tell us that the smaller the car, the more likely you are to be injured or killed in a crash, especially against a bigger car. These studies are not revelations; they affirm the laws of physics. They also tend to violate sense and logic, since they "prove" that cars driven predominantly by young people who are statistically more reckless are also those drivers who own cars that are most dangerous. The danger is in the driver, not in the car. Thus studies show that the Firebird and Camaro are dangerous cars, and the Datsun "Z" cars are the most dangerous of all. The least dangerous cars of all are the biggest Cadillacs. In Chicago people have been assassinated from Cadillacs more often than from any other cars. This is not necessarily a comment on the safety of Cadillacs.

In general, one may say that reckless drivers endanger themselves first, everyone around them second. If such a driver hits you in a car larger than the one you are driving, you are in statistical trouble. That is what one learns from such studies.

2

The Fuel System

CARBURETOR PROBLEMS

If the car starts and stalls more than once or twice, that is not a favorable sign but not necessarily a major symptom. Many new cars stutter that way. In a used car it means probably that the carburetor needs cleaning and adjusting, and you can confirm it by noting engine idle once the car warms up: If the car idles satisfactorily or at least better, you can expect a dirty, worn carburetor. The warm engine expands passageways sufficiently to allow a more normal air-fuel mix to flow through the carburetor.

(Fuel injection systems, if mechanical, may behave in a similar fashion, with similar repairs indicated. Electronic systems can behave that way but are more likely to quit altogether. Hence a driving test won't tell you much about them.)

There are many different types of carburetors, especially including recent General Motors types that are not designed

19

for quick and easy repair (you have to drill into them). But all carburetors can be repaired unless physical damage has occurred. Carburetor work is rather expensive; it's delicate and specialized. That doesn't mean it's terribly difficult, if you know how to follow directions and diagrams. But you can expect to pay for several hours' labor if you buy a car that needs carburetor repairs. Parts cost more. Typically, a carburetor job will be well over $100. If you know how, you can buy a repair kit for $5 and do it yourself.

Any recommendation to fix carburetors is greeted with derisive howls of disbelief, since most mechanics never touch them; they simply replace them. You can do that too, at the price of the rebuilt unit, which is around $75, less in some places. But one can also learn to rebuild, with patience and a few basic tools that cost little, such as a needle-nosed pliers and an assortment of small screwdrivers and wrenches. You will also need some carburetor cleaner such as Gunk (a trade name) and a pot large enough to hold a carburetor while it is being bathed. That isn't comparable to (say) what it takes to boil a missionary in oil; it can be a coffee can.

If you decide to go in for carburetor repair, make a diagram of every hose and connection you remove on the car. Then diagram every puzzling part you remove. For example, Holley carburetors are tricky because they have several pumps that look alike. Normally, the repair kit will contain an exploded diagram of every part in the carburetor, but the diagram won't tell you how to disassemble or assemble. That process must be puzzled out by you, and diagrammed every step of the way. Otherwise you could get into an embarrassing situation where you have to put everything in a box and take it to a garage. The script to get out of such an embarrassment has yet to be written. The cost will be per hour.

Carburetors can endure without attention for many thousands of miles, but they can also commence to balk at quite low mileages. I have repaired a Holley 5210 at 12,000 miles—because it was needed, not because I wanted the experience. Though they are complex, carburetors are fairly convivial components; they do not strand you on a superhighway, and

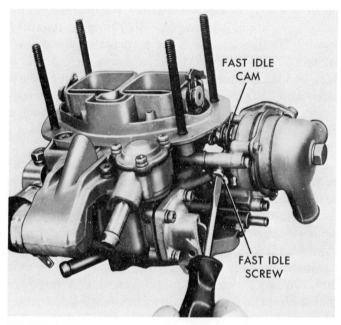

FIGURE 3. A Holley carburetor showing the idle adjustment devices.

they give you fair warning that they require attention. So do mechanical fuel injection systems, found on such cars as late seventies Rabbits.

FUEL PUMP PROBLEMS

Fuel pumps, in contrast to carburetors, are quite hateful, detestable devices. They give you no warning; they can ruin engines as well as strand you. Moreover, test-driving a car provides no clue whatsoever of their condition. Mechanical fuel pumps are inexpensive devices; if you buy a used car with mileage over 25,000, I strongly recommend that you buy a new fuel pump. If you buy a used Omni (or Horizon), I would not only urge you strongly to replace the mechanical fuel pump; I would suggest that Congress pass legislation making it mandatory. The mechanical fuel pumps on these cars have a spring that self-destructs into a scenario of savagery that would elicit disbelief in a soap-opera scriptwriter. It can and does fall into the oil pump, which it ruins. The distributor is next to fall: It can snap off, allowing the rotor to twist slowly in the wind. That ends all possibility of the engine running, only the ending is more sudden than my discourse about it. If the oil pump is ruined—which it may well be—the upper rubbing parts of the engine can be next in line for ruination, including such things as the camshaft. But I believe the point has been made sufficiently.

Does it mean that you shouldn't consider these cars? They are among my top recommendations, because not all such fuel pumps follow the foregoing scenario; indeed, it is statistically rather rare. But it can happen, and because a new pump is inexpensive and easy to install, why take the chance? Meanwhile, these cars are among the best in the world. So, the first thing to do with such a car with mileage above 15,000 or 20,000 is to buy a new fuel pump. In the J. C. Whitney catalog they cost about $12. The chain of wreckage I describe above could cost $1,000. The designer of the fuel pump should properly be hanged, but that is another book. If you started to hang designers of errant car parts, you would have a line that resembled the German Sixth Army walking to Siberia after the surrender at Stalingrad.

I have been talking about mechanical fuel pumps, which are common to most cars on the lots. But electric pumps are found in most imports, and they are becoming familiar enough in Detroit iron. Their advantage is that they don't wear away slowly, losing efficiency as they go; they can be put almost anywhere, whereas the mechanical pump must rub against the camshaft for its power. In theory they can last forever. But cars get very little mileage on theories. Electric pumps are motors; they can wear out and do. Also, their connections can come loose. MGB had a charming design in the late '70s with the fuel pump protruding into the trunk. That's okay; indeed, it's convenient. But the cable that powered it also stuck out, and if you dumped a typical load of sports car gear into the trunk and it landed on that cable, the result was disconnection of the cable and a dead engine that nobody could puzzle out. I mention this not to frighten owners of MGBs, only to frighten slobs. But sports cars are another breed of cat, and the average used-car buyer is not stalking them if statisticians are to be believed.

Since electric pumps can be put anywhere, some terminally sadistic designers have put them in the gas tank. That's where you find them in Vegas, for example. It's like hiding gold in the mattress; reasons can be adduced, but once the robber leaves and the gold is gone, the erstwhile owner begins to ponder alternative hiding places. Because these pumps are electric and can quit one fine day, killing your engine when you most need it, you might wonder what can be done to prevent the disaster. The answer, though not recommended by the

FIGURE 4. Fuel pump and gauge located in gas tank. The Monza is shown.

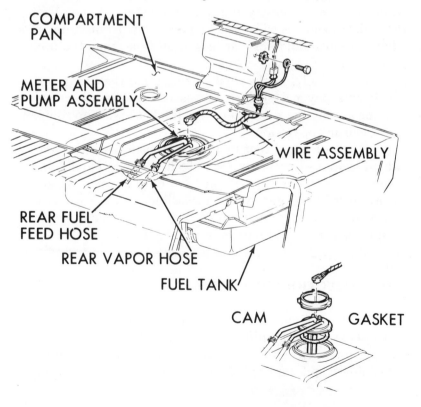

General Motors manuals, is easy. Buy a general-purpose replacement electric pump, attach it to the fender skirt in the engine, attach a rubber hose to the fuel line coming from the dead pump in the gas tank and one to the carburetor inlet, and you are back in business. You must also attach the electrical connection. All this is possible because when the pump fails in the gas tank—and that is true of all such pumps—it fails open, not closed. So, the new pump, though yards away from the gas tank, will soon enough pull out the air from the lines and pull gas through them as precisely as the original pump. The savings—especially if you do it yourself—will be several hundred dollars. Again, is this reason to shun the Vega? Not really. Also, if you are unwilling to try this coronary bypass operation on your own, you can demand it of your mechanic. A GM dealer won't do it; he will assure you that it won't work, it will ruin the engine, destroy the fuel system, and so on. Though any other mechanic will agree to the job, it must be understood that the job should cost far less—half less—than the in-tank operation.

Incidentally, in this bypass operation the new pump in the engine may make bizarre noises at first. That's because it's pulling air through the system, and it takes a while to complete the cleansing operation.

If it is objected that I speak of statistically rare events— which is true—I can only say that if you are the victim, the event becomes in effect 100 percent in frequency. My advice to avoid it is inexpensive and possible, unlike most advice. Statistically rare events that affect you can be as discombobulating as events that happen every day to others.

FUEL INJECTION PROBLEMS

As to fuel injection systems, they are not common yet but soon will appear on most middle-priced cars. These systems replace carburetors with far more gear, hence far greater possibility for breakdown and expense. Mechanical fuel injection systems (those not controlled by computer) aren't much more complicated than carburetors, especially the new GM versions. If you clean them out periodically (or have it done), they will behave much as carburetors. They will warn you when they want overhaul, with familiar symptoms—gasping when you step on the gas instead of surging ahead, leaking, idling roughly, interfering with easy starting, and so on.

Fuel injection systems are generally more expensive to repair than carburetors; so if you are looking for a used car and are making a choice, take the car with the carburetor, all else being equal. Electronic fuel injection systems are found only on the most expensive cars, in which case money may or may not be the deciding factor. But be warned that these systems are more complicated than anything else on your car.

3

Electrical Systems

Electrical systems are the most vexing of all, including as they do the battery, starter, alternator, all the switches and wiring, and all the accessory systems such as air conditioning and lighting, both cosmetic and basic. They are the hardest to diagnose in many cases. They can cause more trouble than everything else. The radio antenna on the left fender of early Rabbits (the 1975–76 models) would develop a rain leak as the anchoring grommet worked loose. Water would trickle down the radio cable into the Rube Goldberg fusebox, rust out some of the switches, and soon your brake lights wouldn't work, the overhead light would quit, and various other electrical interruptions would take place. That fusebox costs about $150 to replace. Alternatively, about the only thing you can do is to wire around it—not all that complex, by the way. (Meanwhile, the J. C. Whitney catalog lists replacement fuseboxes for about $40.)

Electrical failures begin with the battery. When you step on the starter, note how responsive it is. If the turnover rate is slow, that could mean a weak battery. It could also mean a lot of other things, including a worn starter, corrosion on the battery cables, and poor electrical connections elsewhere. The quickest way to test the battery with the starter is to turn on the bright headlights and notice how dim they become when the starter is operating. If they dim a lot, that's a fairly good sign of a weak battery. Of course batteries can also be tested with special equipment. That requires getting to the equipment.

But let's continue testing the battery, forgetting test equipment. Try the turn signals. Sluggish signals can point to a weak battery. If the battery is without filler caps—the no-maintenance type now proliferating—your next step is to check corrosion on the cables and on the battery itself. Weak starting motor turnover can be caused by corrosion. You have to remove the cables from the battery, using simple wrenches. Removing battery cables isn't any more difficult than changing a washer in a simple faucet, but many people would be baffled

FIGURE 5. This person disdains two wrenches, but if the lug nut is corroded and force is applied, the battery could be ruined. Penetrating oil would probably prevent that, but why take the chance?

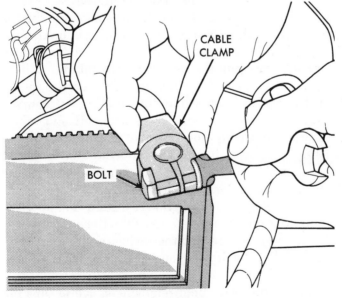

even by that task. The key is to remove the cables without disturbing the battery posts; they're not fragile but no force should be applied to them. So, when you turn the nuts to loosen the lug, use two wrenches—one to hold and absorb the force, the other to turn. Use penetrating oil, and when the fastening nut is opened, take a large screwdriver, put it between the jaws of the lug and open them slightly so that the lug pulls up easily from the battery post.

With a circular file or sandpaper, or even a small knife, clean off the inside of the lug, and the outside battery post. Then use a wet rag on the top of the battery itself to wipe it clean.

Corrosion on the battery top can cause a low-grade short circuit between the positive and negative posts that discharges the battery over time. Replace the lugs and try the starter. If the operation makes no change in the patient, you have at least isolated the two most likely diseases, a weak starter or battery. Batteries don't last much beyond three or four years; starters are judged by mileage (and use). A starter in a car with more than 60,000 miles is a candidate for replacement. However, an abused starter will deteriorate long before that.

Repairing a starter isn't difficult, and you can buy a rebuilt starter for about $30 if you are willing to do the big job: taking out the old one, hauling it to the store, and getting a replacement or getting the one you have rebuilt. Otherwise, starters are expensive. If you simply tell the garage to "fix it," you court a bill for over a hundred dollars. Of course, the cheapest way to go is to take the starter off and rebuild it yourself. Parts probably won't amount to more than a new set of brushes. However, if one starter symptom is present— whirring when the ignition is turned on instead of engaging the flywheel and the motor—you have to replace the gear that does the turning. To do that requires a snap ring pliers, a few other tools, and the ability to follow directions from a manual. Also, it takes a lot of time, and the savings aren't that great. So, if you are willing to do the job we just described, buy the rebuilt starter for $30.

A word to the wise about removing starters: On a big car

the starter is very heavy, and probably located in a place that has about as difficult an access as a harem, with penalty for failure not so drastic, but estimable enough—a broken finger-nail, a bruise or two. On some small cars like Rabbits or Omnis, the starter is easily located. Let starter access be your guide when estimating the amount of work you are prepared to do. The law of diminishing returns sets in quickly.

Battery replacement is familiar enough to most people, who drive into Sears, Penney's, Ward's, and so on, and drive out with a new one. These familiar haunts will test your old battery honestly, and if the problem is in the charging system or the connections, they will tell you. But in many areas you can buy rebuilt batteries for much less. They are basically as good as new. Instead of the $50 to $75 price tag on a new one, the rebuilt saves up to half the amount in some places.

The charging system is a culprit you test by a process of elimination. If the battery tests out to be good, no corrosion is present, and the starter works properly, you then suspect the charging system. One preliminary exam should be given—to the driver. Do you drive short distances, at low speeds, using all the electrical gear on the car—radio, air conditioner or heater, a lot of lights, electric windows, and so on? If so, that's the problem when you suspect low charging. The cure is impossible—new driving habits, but no other cure will work.

If the charging system isn't working properly, the culprits may be the alternator and/or regulator, and in many recent cars the alternator has its regulator built into it. Alternators are usually in the front of the engine, powered by a fan belt. Once charging begins to fail—the red light goes on when it shouldn't—the first thing you do is examine the belt. If it is broken, you know what has to be done. But it could be badly worn and so loose that it simply isn't turning the alternator. A shabby belt turns in shabby performance. That's a very com-mon event in alternator life-style.

But if the problem isn't the driver or the fan belt, the alternator looms up rapidly as a prime contender. It is, after all, a very busy component, supplying electricity for everything that is happening electrically in your car. Unlike the old generator, which went bad only when its brushes or bearings wore out (which was seldom), the alternator has one set of components more fragile and touchy than anything in the generator. These are called *diodes*. They quit with little or no warning (sometimes they emit a squeak). Diodes can self-destruct early in life, or they can outlast the car. Unfortunately you have no choice between these contingencies, and nothing you do can assure obtaining the one instead of the other. That is the nature of most modern electronic "advances."

It is easy to remove an alternator and have it tested. Usually there are only three or four bolts that need loosening or removing, and the alternator can be lifted out of its perch.

FIGURE 6. Diodes and other components inside an alternator by Chevrolet. If your generator warning light remains on when you turn off the ignition key, it is usually a sign of a defective diode.

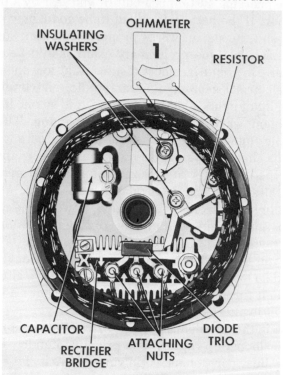

Those alternators that reside down below are usually approachable from the bottom of the car, entailing only the inconvenience of doing the work underneath. The alternator is not terribly heavy, like the starter, so its removal is rather dainty as these things are judged.

It is hard to recommend replacement of ailing diodes, simply because the job is easily botched. Also, you can buy rebuilt alternators for about $35. Additionally, brushes often need replacement, and though that's fairly easy, a lot of tiny parts are present in an alternator that are easily lost or misplaced. On the other hand, new alternators will cost at least $100, if you can get to the garage and utter that costly phrase "fix it."

A separate regulator is inexpensive in most modern cars. The alternator test will eliminate or confirm a defective regulator: If the alternator is good, the regulator almost certainly is not. Regulators, much less costly, endure perversely compared with alternators.

Electrical systems have switches, lights, and wiring systems. They also have fuseboxes, relays, sensors, and connectors. All these components—many of them tiny—wear out, and some of them strand you when they do. A silly $2 resistor, such as you find in most Chryslers, perched on the firewall, can kill ignition if it breaks.

The new electronic ignition systems, with their sensors, microprocessors, and coils, are also part of the electrical system, since they run on electricity—or rather they control the electrical system. In many ways they are the most perverse of all systems that plague a car owner. They are "sudden death" systems. They are not alone; plenty of mechanical systems also fall into that dismal, dangerous category. The fact is, a car is a brigand, stealthily waiting to assault you when you least expect it. The electronic systems, and the electrical systems they control, are only part of the problem. To be sure, they do replace more reliable systems; for example, mechanical distributors wore out but didn't strand you unless you turned a deaf ear to their symptoms. And carburetors of the old school, without electronic controls, also behaved with much greater civility.

But modernity will not be denied. Modern horrors are considered more desirable by designing engineers than ancient civilities. Every electrical-electronic system that replaces any mechanical system, or is put in control of that system, introduces an element of instability. That arises because a visual inspection can tell you nothing about the condition of the new system. No matter how expert your eye, a mere visual inspection of sensors, coils, microprocessors, wire cables and clusters, and all the other paraphernalia of the modern car won't give you a clue to subsequent behavior, however atrocious. In general, the worse the behavior, the more elaborate and devious the justification for it. Strictly speaking, one cannot charge electronic ignition and its perpetrators with criminal behavior, but when it strands you on the south side of Chicago, it is at least an accessory after the fact. Engineers can prove, with charts and statistics, that the new electronic gear gets better mileage, requires fewer adjustments and maintenance procedures, and has other advantages. As noted previously, they are too well hidden.

Does that mean that inspection of a used car of recent vintage is of no use when it comes to these systems? Inspect mileages. If an alternator has gone 60,000 miles without incident, it is due for new brushes—a minor operation. In many makes it can be done without taking anything apart, other than the brush assemblies. All removable ignition parts should be replaced periodically—including control modules, rotors, sensors, distributor caps, and even coils. Only cracks in the distributor cap can be seen, and these with difficulty, in a bright light by a practiced eye. All the other components present an innocent facade. But the innocence is mocking; you cannot trust any of these devices. Unfortunately, no mileages can be trusted either. Some control modules go on forever; others die very quickly. So, too, with the other parts of the system.

Wiring systems and fuseboxes are maddening. The fat wiring harnesses, and their foolproof connectors and fasteners, give off a sense of well-being that is almost redoubtable. Who could suspect them? But vibration and dirt take their toll of every engine component, including wiring. Water can leak into places that house fuseboxes and connectors, and it will ruin everything, given half a chance. And saltwater, which you get in winter, doesn't even need a half chance.

In this connection beware especially of the Rabbit and its 1975-and-later fusebox, as previously noted. How can you tell about it? Not easily. You must peek up under the dash by the steering column, unlatch the fusebox, and drop it forward. Using a flashlight, look into its insides for signs of rust. Pull out the several relay switches—they plug in—and look for rust. If rust is there, beware.

Most fuseboxes are not so diabolical. The MGB, for example, is simplicity itself: a small box on the fender skirt inside the engine on the passenger side.

Wiring harnesses are not immortal, but you can't go around replacing them on suspicion. You can examine those that run across or around the engine for severe burn spots on the insulation. Those will have to be replaced. Otherwise, you get what you see. The vast mass of connectors and relays, switches and wire harnesses, must be bought on faith. Thanks to auto designers, faith is not the first thing that springs to one's mind when one is contemplating a used car.

It should be noted that tracking down electrical problems is tedious and time consuming, even for experts. So electrical work tends to be more expensive than other kinds, especially when you have to replace a major electrical component. Minor components, such as light bulbs and even headlights are best replaced by you at home. Much expense can be saved if you are willing to use a screwdriver and small wrench—and follow directions. In buying a car, it goes without saying that you should test all the lights, radio, heater, air conditioner, electric windows if any and any other electrical gadgets on the car. A light or a piece of electrical equipment that does not work may mean nothing beyond itself. But it can also mean trouble elsewhere that could mount up.

It should be noted that most professional mechanics look

first at electrical connections, which are easily jarred loose or corroded, before proceeding to make equipment tests. The rankest amateur can look at connections, as we've seen with battery lugs, and take a piece of sandpaper to them. Miracle cures are often effected this way.

One set of cables does require regular replacement: the spark plug cables. Every 15,000 miles or so is time enough, unless inspection reveals insulation wear, burn, and tear. Defective cables interfere with engine firing, thereby causing weird engine behavior. Any car can have such cables, and they are candidates for inspection, along with tires, battery, starter, lights, and other "up front" components. However, in order to inspect these cables properly, you have to pull them off. Problems, problems. Twist them before pulling, so as to loosen any sticking between cable and plug. Don't pull on the cable; pull on the boot at the plug. Otherwise you'll ruin the cable.

Defective cables sometimes glow in the dark; they give off sparks, which reflect the fact that they are short-circuiting, or "arcing," hence not delivering electricity to the plug. You can see that if you run the engine in the dark with the hood open. However, the same symptoms can be caused by other components, especially the distributor cap. When a hairline crack occurs in the cap, it will cause arcing and worse—a cracked distributor cap can prevent firing altogether. However, it isn't likely that a used car would have such a problem. But worn spark plug cables are something else; if they aren't badly battered, they probably won't be replaced by the dealer.

Electrical repairs, like all others, vary from place to place and depend ultimately on hourly rates. They are highest at dealer garages, lowest at gas stations and some private garages. But some repairs won't be made by the lower-priced garages, especially by gas station mechanics, who, though they may be at least as skilled as dealer mechanics, may not have enough equipment for some tasks.

Electric windows, for example, are notoriously difficult to repair in some cases—not in all. The job is time consuming and laborious because of the management of the heavy spring and the awkward places for getting at the components and

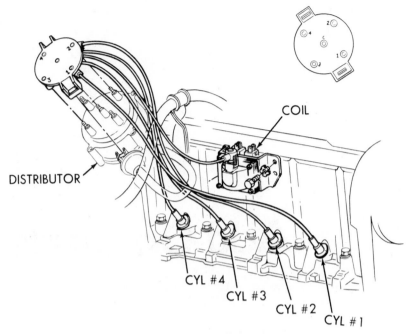

FIGURE 7. Components of a Chevrolet, High Energy Ignition (HEI) system, on a four-cylinder engine. Shown are spark plug cables, coil, and distributor.

electrical connections. Unless you have a few special tools, the job gets very expensive, and even with them it becomes costly if the motor needs replacement—which it often does. The motor costs about $50; the labor could be twice that.

4

Add-On Costs

No relationship with a garage gets as sticky as that between it
and the customer over repairs, especially when the customer
looks at the long list of parts that get replaced.

If you go in for a single job—say engine tuneup—at a
garage, lured by the price, $59.95 special, parts extra, and
whistle cheerfully before you get the bill, you will be at least
outraged at the additional costs. Homicides have been caused
by the situation. What has happened here? Is it merely a
communications gap?

It is worse; it is the add-on parts routine. It produces a
gap more vicious than communication. Some of it is justified.
You can expect to buy a new set of spark plugs, and pay the
highest retail price—say about $2 or more each, instead of the
discount store price of 80 cents or so. Then, if your car has
electronic ignition, which it probably has if it was built in 1975
or later, the sticky part of the equation rears its ugly head. In a
GM car you will probably be stuck for a control module—
priced anywhere from $35 to $50—possibly a sensor with a

price tag not much lower than the module but involving taking the distributor apart hence an added $50 for labor. You might pay $15 or $20 for a rotor and distributor cap, whereas you could buy them yourself for half that price and install them in a few minutes. There is no telling how many other parts the garage might foist on you, some of which might have actually required replacement but most of which would have had only marginal problems or, in some cases, have been perfectly fine. For example, a garage will never clean spark plugs, and if they are merely fouled from oil or gas, you will pay for new ones. Here, the garage probably is on your side. They would charge you $2 to clean each old plug and you would still have old plugs.

The carburetor might not behave to specifications. Here they would be obligated to call you for permission because labor would cost a minimum of $50 and a lot more in some cases, and parts would cost similar amounts. So that $59.95 special is already over $200 and going up. It could escalate into a $400 bill.

Of course, you could do all the work yourself and pay about $35 worth of parts, assuming that all are needed. That's always a questionable assumption. Service managers have one major talent: selling extra parts and labor.

Some repairs come with a fixed price—usually high. The bill for an automatic transmission repair usually is posted and rarely would need to go above the promised price, since transmissions are self-contained units. But transmissions are not typical components; they have little to do with the rest of the car. They merely pass on what the engine does. Brakes, which are among the most frequently repaired systems, are also trickily priced. They too often come with specific price tags, but the bill you pay bears little relation to the promised amount. That's because brakes are like ignition systems: They use a lot of parts and labor, and pads or linings are rarely the whole story. You can pay up to $200 for a brake job when rotors and cylinders need replacement or heavy work. Any car with brake problems should have a correspondingly lower asking price. The discount .should take note of the cost of those added parts and labor—the cylinders, rotors, and so on.

So, when you price any used car, bear in mind the possible add-on costs for any repairs you know about. The costs of such repairs can easily double and triple the posted "special" price, and that is especially true of electrical parts, which are hard to see.

5

Engine and Transmission

ENGINE PROBLEMS

Anything done to the inside of an engine, except the most superficial valve lash adjustment, begins at around $250. That includes any work that involves the valves, pistons, camshaft, crankshaft, and bearings. These basic engine components require hours of labor to expose and service; the parts themselves quickly add up to imposing costs. A camshaft can cost $150 to $200, and the labor to replace it can cost almost as much. Push rods, valve lifters, rocker assemblies, and gaskets all contribute heavily to engine repair costs. Pumps around the engine—fuel, oil, steering—are terribly expensive in some cases, though not in all. But an oil pump is expensive simply because the engine oil pan must be dropped to get at the pump, and in many cars you have to raise the engine to remove the oil pan and sometimes remove steering and suspension parts as well.

Oil leaks are among the most common engine repairs. If

FIGURE 8. A typical V-8 engine by Plymouth with power steering pump (below fan), air conditioning (top front), starting motor (bottom rear), carburetor, and distributor (top middle and rear).

only gaskets are involved, the costs are relatively low: $25 to $50. But if oil is getting past the valve push rods and into the combustion chamber, the problem is much more expensive. If oil is being pushed past the piston rings, the problem is even worse. Now we are talking about an engine overhaul, and the price varies from about $500 to about $1,500, depending on what is done—that is, how many parts are replaced.

How can you tell what is needed? Engines can be deceptive. Wear in any of the components of the valve train decreases engine efficiency. Valves, valve springs, lifters, guides, and push rods, when worn, cause sluggish behavior. But so can engine timing and carburetion that aren't correct, to say nothing of worn ignition parts. So, one goes first to those systems before condemning an engine. But if fuel and ignition systems are exonerated, one suspects internal engine wear.

Several types of internal engine work may be distinguished. There is the simple, usually inexpensive valve lash adjustment on those engines that require it—usually small, four-cylinder types—and upper and lower pan gasket replacements, also not very expensive for most cars. Then there is valve train work—upper engine. Finally, the complete overhaul rings the biggest cost bell.

A trail of exhaust smoke means oil is burning—a basic clue to internal engine wear. If the oil is pushed into the combustion chamber past the rings, it means a total overhaul usually. A compression test will tell that tale. If the fault is above the rings and in the valve train, the job is less costly. Those are the alternatives, and you can suspect any engine with more than 65,000 miles of being susceptible to either problem. You also subtract the possible costs from the price of the car. But compression tests to reveal ring wear are not routinely given. Garages will charge for such a test. In view of the large sums involved, it is worth the small sum for the test. Consider it a tiny investment: about $15.

Sluggish engine performance in a driving test begins when you turn the ignition key. Hard starting may be a symptom of poor compression—though one cannot rule out ignition and fuel problems. How can that be done on a used-car lot? If you ask questions about ignition and fuel systems, you *may* find some answers. But you can make superficial examinations about starting yourself. You assess battery and starter condition. Then look at spark plug cables. Are they worn and shabby, or are they new? Look at the distributor cap; is it old and greasy or new and shiny? If there are new parts around the engine in the fuel and ignition systems, that's evidence you can rule out those systems, though it's not conclusive; only testing equipment can make that final determination.

Engine noises are also good clues to engine condition. Noisy valve lifters make a characteristic clatter that is usually correctable with either valve lash adjustment or new lifters. But lifters are an expensive operation. So, insist on a valve adjustment if you contemplate buying a car with a noisy engine. If that is impossible, either make a lower offer or don't buy the car at all. Moreover, any noise from an engine indicates some problem, even if it's nothing more than a loose fan belt, a squeaky alternator, or a water pump in the throes of disintegration. These are all estimable woes, once past the fan belt, but they don't affect internal engine performance. They should be ruled out: The alternator by following those steps we have noted, the water pump by examining it for leaks (look for droplets of antifreeze) and jiggling it around to determine if the pump pulley is solid. (If you can push the pulley around at all, the pump is almost certainly defective.) Water pumps usually reside just behind the radiator, though plenty of them are found elsewhere, all VW type engines put them down below on the passenger side, for example.

Thumping noises from an engine mean bearing damage, or piston and other possibly disqualifying problems. *Don't buy* such a car.

Engines can give off all kinds of warning noises, from squeaks and squeals to grinding or breaking sounds. In the latter category, the kind of road disaster that I mentioned in connection with Omni and Horizon is accompanied by a noise, but it happens quickly and there's no precaution you can take except the one I have specified: buying a new fuel pump once the mileage mounts up. The engine will simply not run, whereas a second before it was running flawlessly.

Squeaks usually come from belted components, such as the fuel, water, steering, and other mechanical pumps. Air pumps, found on many cars in emission control systems, squeak before they destruct. Some of these pumps are horribly expensive; Rabbit, for example, will set you back $256 for a new one. Of course you can bypass the air pump, and the car will run almost as well, though the absence of the pump will have a slightly adverse effect on idle and acceleration (it will also raise emissions slightly), but otherwise you can go on as if nothing had happened. Used pumps can be bought for about $50, and they are easily installed.

Squeaks also signify an alternator that may be in the process of wearing out diodes, brushes, or bearings. Any old alternator (one with heavy mileage) is a candidate. But squeaking components rarely strand you. Even a dying alternator won't stop the engine immediately, though you'd better get to

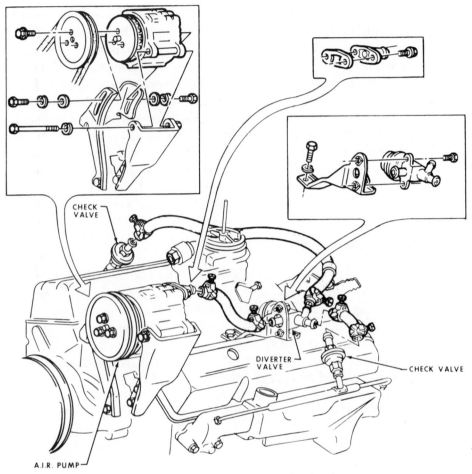

CHECK VALVE

DIVERTER VALVE

CHECK VALVE

A.I.R. PUMP

FIGURE 9. An emission control system on an engine, showing the air pump and other components.

a garage pronto, since the battery will discharge sooner or later, in a matter of an hour or less.

Any loose belt can cause squeaks, and most engines have several belts: air conditioner, steering pump, water pump, alternator, and fan. The test for a loose belt is to push on it. The belt shouldn't push in much more than half an inch. Any belt that does needs either replacement or tightening.

Electric fuel pumps can make strange noises—anything

from gurgling to whirring. Strictly speaking, these noises have nothing to do with the insides of the engine, but they *do* affect its operation. It is important to recognize them for what they are and not confuse them with engine symptoms. Engine noises are caused by wear, which is usually caused by heavy mileage and/or poor maintenance, the key to which is the failure to make regular oil changes. Noises from components outside the engine don't have a single cause, so they tend to be different from one another and from internal engine sounds. Also, internal engine sounds are muffled and often decrease after the engine warms up. Sticking valve lifters, for example, may exhibit such behavior and vanish after warm-up.

OIL LEAKING AND BURNING

Oil seems to leak from engines with the ease of babies soiling diapers, and it isn't confined to leaks from engines; transmissions and rear axles can also suffer this malady. Even fairly new cars have these messy problems. So, what's a used-car buyer supposed to do?

First, keep the problem in perspective. A few drops of oil on the ground or garage floor are not cause for panic. Every leaking grease or oil source contains hundreds of thousands of drops and a few can be spared. But when the leaking becomes worse than a few droplets, the problem must be confronted.

Engine Leaks

Engine leaks come basically from two sources: the gaskets at the top and bottom of the engine, less often from the oil filter gasket or the gasket at the fuel pump or from the various electrical sensors plugged into the engine. Correcting leaks is difficult and expensive only from the bottom engine oil sump gasket. All the others are fairly easily corrected, hence inexpensive. But sometimes gasket replacement doesn't do the job.

That happens when oil is being blown or otherwise forced out of the oil chambers and galleys because of worn rings, valve guides, lifters, and valves. In such a situation, no gasket will hold the oil. So, leaking oil from the engine is not necessarily benign; it may be one more sign of basic engine wear. Thus signs of oil leaks from the engine must be examined carefully and are one more important reason for a compression test.

Some oil leaks are caused by a head gasket that leaks not because of worn valves and rings but because of some unusual event, such as overheating or loose head bolts. That can sometimes be corrected simply by tightening the head bolts to the specified torque. At other times, correction can only be effected by removing the head and machining it for warp—a defect in the engine caused by overheating. This is a costly repair but a necessary one. The job takes several hours, plus the machine shop work. It cannot be done for less than $200 and it could be more, depending on how difficult it is to remove the head.

On the other hand, leaks from the pan gasket on top—the rocker pan—can be quickly and inexpensively cured; don't pay much more than $25 for this job.

Are some cars more, or less, prone to oil leaks? It has nothing to do with make or model and everything to do with engine design and wear. The bigger the engine—the greater the number of cylinders—the more surfaces there are to leak oil. But the big engine is no more likely to leak oil because of design than the smallest four-cylinder, allowing for the larger surfaces. However, some cosmetic designs minimize oil leaks in such cars as Audi, Mercedes, and other expensive cars. They use sturdier gasket fittings, or extra components to enhance the sealing ability of the gaskets. These are superficial but effective tactics. Not many manufacturers resort to them. Too bad.

Transmission Leaks

Transmissions are also favorite places for oil leaks to occur. That is true of both automatic and stick shift transmissions. The problem is much less likely to occur in the stick shift, where it is less costly to repair. Oil seals in automatic transmissions aren't terribly costly to repair; they don't cost as much as a transmission overhaul, but you can expect a price tag up to $175 for installing new seals.

You can see transmission oil leaks because of the color of the oil: It's reddish purple. But it isn't that simple to discover, and it would be deceptive to pretend that all you have to do is peek underneath the transmission. For one thing, oil can also leak out of the transmission oil pan through the gasket. That's an easy repair to make. If oil leaks there, you won't be able to distinguish it from the leaks around the seals. In any event, don't give up on a car solely because of transmission oil leaks.

TRANSMISSION AND CLUTCH PROBLEMS

However, the transmission itself is another story. A transmission that doesn't shift effortlessly, smoothly, and flawlessly is telling you of expensive trouble ahead. That is especially true of an automatic, though a stick shift is hardly less expensive to repair. We are talking about prices of $300 to $600 nowadays, though some problems can be fixed for less. In a test drive the transmission and, in a stick shift, the clutch should be among the most carefully assessed items. An automatic transmission should be tested through every shifting possibility, especially reverse. If it's a Ford automatic, put the shift lever in "Park," jiggle the accelerator, and open and bang the door. You're looking for the famous self-shift motion of the Ford automatic that consumer groups have contended is literally murderous. Don't forget that the Ford shift is also found on Mercury and Lincoln models, but it is not found on Fords manufactured overseas. On this automatic the shift lever drops into reverse unaided by you *unless* it is locked properly. The use of the accelerator and the banging of the door are cited as sufficient force to jiggle the lever out of its "Park" slot if it isn't anchored securely. So, how do you secure the transmission? Make one extra push up and in on the lever—a motion *not* required by other automatics and hence regarded by critics as cause for holding Ford responsible for an accident-prone product. It is hard to agree with the critics on this matter. God did not create all his children in the image of General Motors shifters. However, some of these levers are more prone to the self-shift than others, and that is what you are looking for, since it means the possibility of excessive wear is present.

When you test an automatic, you are looking for flaws in shifting. Ask yourself if the engine races at some point in the shift process. The old General Motors automatic of the early 1970s, which had only two forward shifts, would race the engine (that is, disconnect the engine from the transmission) going around a bend with low oil levels in the transmission. Some of these cars are still around.

Does the transmission balk at any point? Is reverse smooth and without noticeable hitch? Does the transmission jerk at any point? Does it respond instantly to the accelerator? (If it doesn't, that could be caused by the engine, too.)

With a stick shift you must also be concerned with the clutch. In these days a clutch overhaul is as expensive as anything you can do to a transmission. However, stick shift symptoms often obscure the origin of flaws: Is it the clutch or is it the transmission? Neither is desirable. Any flaw in shifting or performance that is traceable to clutch or transmission could mean an overhaul, and we're talking about $250-to-$500 price tags.

In front-engine rear-drive cars, the drive shaft can have universal-joint wear that causes clunking and other symptoms. These should not be confused with transmission problems, and they are much less costly to repair. However, a rear axle that needs much work *is* expensive. Its symptoms are mostly noise—grinding of expensive, delicate gears. Look around the rear axle for grease and oil leaks. Dry gears, thanks to leaks, are soon ruined gears. The leaks can be found both at the wheels and in the center of the axle—that bulging chamber. You look behind the wheels. We'll have more to say about that in the discussion of brakes.

6

Brakes and Suspension System

For about forty years Detroit made brakes and suspension systems as if they were carved in stone, using the front-engine rear-drive configuration that dictated the way you suspended and braked. When front drive started to elbow its way forward, the rules changed. Soon, front drive will sweep the boards and you can kiss the old configurations good-bye. This changeover will harbor causes for mixed emotions. The new front drive vastly simplifies suspension of cars in some ways and complicates it in others. Obviously, if you add power to wheels that formerly were required only to steer themselves, you add big complications. That is what front drive does. But the new suspension system that came along, courtesy of the Mac-Pherson strut, made it possible to eliminate a ton of linkage, joints, and various paraphernalia, all of which wore out regularly. However, the new strut system introduced these penalties: far costlier shock absorbers and front bearings. Detroit suspension systems made shock absorber replacement as common and inexpensive as anything you can do to a car. The strut reverses that equation: If you drive a used car with strut suspension, which has the usual worn shock absorber symptoms (front end wobble and sway, drift, tire wear, and so on), be prepared to pay a whopping bill—up to $200 and over.

FIGURE 10. A MacPherson strut suspension showing all brake, strut, steering, and fastening details.

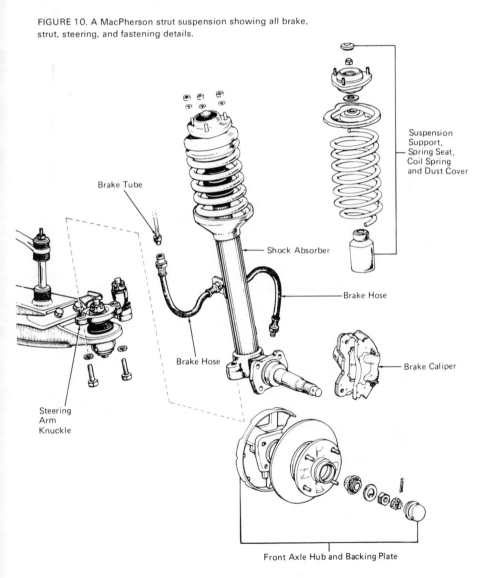

Suspension Support, Spring Seat, Coil Spring and Dust Cover

Brake Tube

Shock Absorber

Brake Hose

Brake Hose

Brake Caliper

Steering Arm Knuckle

Front Axle Hub and Backing Plate

That's because both parts and labor are far more expensive. Bearing replacement is much costlier. Figure $150 in many cases, but subtract the big bills attendant on the various failures of bushings, linkage, idler arms, pitman arms, and all the other front-end wear points. The rear suspension systems of the front-drive cars are simplicity itself. Here, too, you eliminate a ton of costly gear(s). And you don't have to add any expensive components or devices. All is simple.

If you buy an older Detroit car, all suspension components, including upper and lower control arm bushings, are likely wear points. Typically these bushings wear out above 75,000 miles. Wear symptoms are clunking noises in the front end, tire wear on one side, and inability to correct alignment. These bushings have rubber cases that wear out, down to the metal. Metal then clunks against metal as the arms move up and down. But other front-end components have similar effects, especially the idler and pitman arms, which anchor steering linkage. Front-end work of these kinds can get pretty expensive, because a typical job will turn up a lot of other jobs. Ball joints, for example, that wear out fairly often, usually take other components with them. Ball joints cost from $60 to $100 to replace, by themselves. When you add some of the devices that usually expire with these joints, you can spend a lot of money on a front end. So beware of older Detroit iron. Or check out the front suspension system carefully.

That's not so easily done. Visual inspection won't tell you much. Everything depends on what happens during driving— also what has happened to the tires. Examine the tires for uneven wear. That's a vital clue. Then drive over some rough surfaces and move the car around; don't drive carefully. Bushing noises will show up on a sudden wrench of the suspension system, as when you drive over a bump of some sort. Take a high driveway head on, and give the car a good bang.

You can sometimes get information about control arms by opening the hood and looking at the upper control arms. Typically they will be concealed by a flapping rubber or fiber skirt on the inner fender wall. Pull up the skirt and look at the bushings, which are at each end of the axlelike device that you can see moving when you push down on the car. If you see strands of rubber straying loosely out of these devices, you can be sure the bushings need replacement. The job is expensive, and both sides will need it if one does. Figure from $75 to $125 at least. (These would be small garage or gas station prices; big-city dealer garages would almost double that price range.)

You may wonder whether all used cars fit these strictures. Some foreign cars—Fiats and others—use strut suspensions in front, even though they may not be front-drive cars. And some cars use strut suspension all around. But these configurations don't change the specific symptoms involved; struts do their thing whether on front or rear or whatever else is going on around them. They merely have an easier time of it when they don't have to contend with power wheels along with steering. Strains on them are less.

Brake lore runs deep in garage routines. People complain about brakes more than about any other part of the car. Reason enough: They stand between the driver and destiny. Nowadays brakes are all dual systems: If one self-destructs, the other system will stop the car. It may pull a little, but it will do the job.

Brakes work by means of friction between pad and rotor or lining and drum. That means constant, inevitable wear. Linings and pads last for 12,000 to 50,000 miles. Why the disparity? You—the driver. A heavy foot on the pedal condemns the linings, rotors, and drums to an early grave; a light, solicitous foot expands brake life enormously.

But brake systems also include master cylinders, brake lines, and wheel cylinders. And rear brakes must contend with oil seals between brakes and axles that develop leaks and ruin rear lining in cars with rear axles turning the wheels. So brakes live the perils of Pauline, with you as a silent partner.

What does test driving tell you about brakes? Quite a bit, but far from the whole story. Begin at the beginning, the parking brake. When you enter the car, check out the brake. Is it on? If the car is on a hill, see if the parking brake holds. If it doesn't, that probably means that the rear linings are no good.

That won't affect stopping if the front brakes are okay, since they do about 85 percent of the job. A lot of people will let rear brakes go to rack and ruin for that reason. If you live in San Francisco, however, you do not have such an option. In Chicago parking brakes are rarely needed.

Brakes can stop a car even when they are almost completely worthless; they can fail to stop a car though they may be almost flawless. If a master cylinder fails to work, the brakes will fail even if all other aspects of the systems are perfectly good. For these quixotic reasons brakes are not regarded as the most perfect systems imaginable, but nobody has come forward with a better idea.

If brakes pull to one side, that means either faulty linings or pads, damaged rotors or drums, wheel cylinders that need rebuilding, or sticking components in the disk caliper, also fluid lines with blockage somewhere. If linings on disk pads or drum systems are worn, they will squeak, pull, buckle, stop with a shudder, make grinding noises if worn enough to touch the metal of the rotor or drum, or fail to stop in the expected distance. Most cars nowadays have warning signals built in to tell you when the pads or linings need replacement on the front wheels. But as they approach the point where the signal is activated, they can exhibit a lot of the symptoms just described. And, of course, the signal doesn't tell you anything else about the brakes; they can be in the process of collapsing totally, and the signal won't have anything to say.

Worn pads or linings also show up in pedal travel. If you have to push the pedal down too far, that's a good sign of excessive wear. But it could also be caused by fluid loss. So brakes are complex. I have not even mentioned the several valves in systems that equalize braking force and effort; I haven't mentioned the power brake devices, which consist of a series of diaphragms, plates, springs, and rods all activated by engine vacuum pressure. These, too, can fail, though power brake devices are more or less foolproof and simple. The proportioning and metering valves are pretty tough customers also, but they can fail and bollix up the system.

Are some cars better off in the brake department? No,

because brakes are international; they are all made by a few companies, such as Bendix. Any salesman who claims superiority for his brakes over somebody else's knows little about brakes or is pulling your leg.

You can spend several hundred dollars repairing brake systems, so be wary of a car that seems to have brake troubles.

In addition to the testing of brakes during the test drive of a car, it makes sense to look on the insides of the four wheels for signs of fluid leaks. Oil or grease on the inside of the brakes means trouble. In front, it means caliper or cylinder rebuilding; in back, it means cylinder and possibly oil seal replacement. These can get expensive—$100 or more.

FIGURE 11. A GM drum brake assembly showing parking brake details on rear wheel.

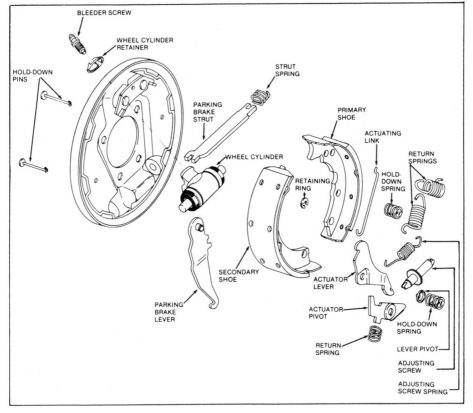

Parking brake problems can mean nothing more than an adjustment—simple tightening, costing virtually nothing. But if the problem is in the oil seals of the axle or the wheel cylinders of the brakes, the problem is big and expensive. Abuse plus mileage are the causes of brake problems. So add yet another system that you must suspect once the mileage gets over 60,000, since you can't expect to check up on the driving habits of all previous owners of such a car.

Should you eliminate from consideration a car that passes all other tests? Probably not. The chances of a car needing all the components of a brake system are virtually nil. What is usually needed is a new set of linings and/or pads, possibly drums or rotors smoothed out ("turned"). That job shouldn't cost more than about $70 or so. It should rarely be necessary to buy new rotors or drums, and these are the most expensive parts of the system. Also, used rotors and drums may often be available, though the typical garage won't use them, preferring the higher profitability in the new parts. Used parts are mostly meant for the do-it-yourself mechanic.

The rebuilding of wheel and master cylinders shouldn't be more than about $20 per wheel if you are also buying relining. Master cylinders are something else. If you can find a mechanic willing to rebuild instead of replace, the job should cost no more than $50. But a brand-new one would cost about $75, installed. And I have heard about a $140 bill on an import. The fact is, the parts that need replacement in a master cylinder can be bought for $15 or $20 and installed in about a half hour. Rebuilding calipers in disk brakes are more expensive; fortunately, they rarely require it. Resist any mechanic who tries to sell you such a job unless he can show you the leaks that make it mandatory. (You can see them yourself by checking behind the wheels and at the bottom of the brakes.)

Squeaky brakes are a law unto themselves. Brakes squeak when they have fundamental problems; they squeak when they have no problems at all. So they are like cats. Just as you can't cure squeaks in cats, so your best efforts with brakes will usually have similar consequences: none. You can cure some

squeaks by replacing linings or pads, even though they don't
need it from wear. What happens is that they become "glazed"
or hardened from long, tough use, and even though they aren't
worn down to the nub, the only way to get rid of the squeak is
to get rid of the lining or pad. Squeaks are also caused by
drums and rotors that are out of line—that is, they need
"truing up." That can be expensive or not, depending on how
much room there is left on the rotor or drum for the correct
execution of the "truing" process, which consists of removing
enough metal from the offending surfaces to get the whole
thing straightened out.

Squeaks also are caused by grease spots on the linings
and pads or by dirt particles getting embedded into the fibers
of the linings. It isn't as easy as it sounds to rid the brakes of
these annoyances. Also, such squeaks often are intermittent:
Now you hear them, now you don't. So, in the absence of any
other major symptom, squeaks in a set of brakes alone are not
enough to make you give up on a used car. Unless it can be
shown that the squeaks are caused by some major malfunction,
which isn't likely, the squeaks should be overlooked in assessing
a car. They don't interfere with braking, unless they come from
very low pads or linings, in which case the noises will be more
like grinding than like squeaking. Then you must take action,
and that would be the rare squeak.

Other noises include shuddering and clunking noises.
Shuddering noises when brakes are applied are caused by
locking up, or sudden sticking. That means there is something
wrong with the braking surfaces and/or the lines. It rarely
happens with good linings and metal surfaces. Clunking usually
isn't the fault of brakes but what the braking process disturbs.
Usually that means bushings. However, calipers (disk brake
housing) can develop clunking, especially on older Chrysler
brakes and others with the same configurations. What happens
is that antirattle springs and other devices don't do their duty.
Chrysler uses an antirattle plate-*cum*-retainer on top of the
pads. Though the design seems foolproof, Murphy's law can yet
apply: Anything that can go wrong will. What happens is that as
pads wear down, caliper surfaces stick to one another as they

move under brake pressure. New pads and greasing of moving caliper surfaces usually cure the problem quite easily.

Usually, however, clunking is not in brakes but in the bushings, and especially where it hurts—financially—in the control arms.

Brake squealing is merely an aggravated form of brake squeaking. The causes of squeaking account for squealing; so do the cures.

Low pedal is always caused by worn linings and pads and/or low amounts of oil in the master cylinder. The latter is caused by leaks either at the master cylinder, or in the wheel cylinders, or less often in the lines. Leaks in brake lines used to be deadly and are a favorite dramatic device on television crime shows, where the assassin cuts the neoprene lines. However, the metal lines that go from the master cylinder to the wheels can rust out after so long a time or merely from rust formations that happen outside any time frame. These will eat through the metal. So it is wise, even though it's a pain, to go beneath the car and examine the brake metal lines every year or so for rust. They aren't supposed to rust; that is, they are made of "rust-proof" metals. But dikes aren't supposed to break, dams to leak. Remember the Jamestown flood; the Dutch boy and his finger?

In every case, however, unlike the instances of terminal rust damage, brakes can be repaired, and it makes economic and mechanical sense to do so. Even if you have to replace every component in the system—an extremely unlikely possibility— you might still find the bottom line to be in your favor, assuming that you could get the cost discounted from the buying price and knew a mechanic who would scrounge for used parts. Of course, if you could do the job yourself, you would save about 90 percent. It isn't all that difficult; brake repair is fairly easy if you omit one or two of the more arcane procedures (rebuilding calipers and replacing oil seals in rear axles—two low-frequency disasters).

7

Rusty Questions

Recalls by the U.S. government are of interest to used-car buyers, but it isn't always possible to sort out political from mechanical problems. Mid-seventies Chrysler products, for example, were recalled for front fender rust damage, but plenty of other cars had worse fender rust, yet they weren't recalled. Similar rust damage in Toyotas, for example, didn't cause a recall. Early Vegas and Hondas had worse rust damage and weren't recalled. But there have been so many recalls that you couldn't buy a car if you worried about it.

Thus far we've been talking about reasons for buying a used car cautiously or not at all. But most car buying is done on impulse based solely on appearance and on accessories. So if you fall into the category of the impulse buyer—and only you can know that—you won't put much faith in the kind of flaw analysis preceding. But the fancy gadgets won't be soothing if they don't work or cost huge sums to repair that ruin your budget, and the shiny exterior might conceal terminal rust or rust that will cost hundreds of dollars to repair. So even the most resolute of impulse buyers—those who scorn systematic advice—should at least turn on the stereo and air conditioner and peek below the surfaces in quest of rust. All cars will have rust; the question is how much and where?

Cars over three or four years of age will have body rust in various degrees of virulence. Expect to find such rust in trunks and along lower panels, in doors, and at the bottoms of all fenders. In the trunks rust usually starts with deteriorated rear window gaskets and cement. The rain trickles into the trunk and settles there, rusting out rear fenders and the floor of the trunk itself. This kind of rust can turn a car into junk if it is not stopped in time, and it can be stopped. But the price can be very high (unless you are willing to tackle the job yourself, when it becomes very cheap—the price of materials, which is about $30, and your labor, whatever that is worth in your view). Rust damage, as we will see, is one of the chief problems in used cars, with engine and transmission running a close second and third. It is costly to repair, when it is done professionally, and is the one repair that anyone can do, given the willingness to tackle it, since it requires no mechanical talent whatsoever. Body work, indeed, is more closely related to metal sculpture than to auto repair. If you have ever wanted to sculpt, now is the time to learn and save a ton of money on a used car.

The majority of cars fall between the smallest cars and largest, both domestic makes and foreign, including the very latest GM front-drive intermediates. Rust damage will be found on any car—domestic or foreign—that is over two or three years old. Is it "planned obsolescence"? Unplanned obsolescence would be closer to the mark. Detroit has not exerted itself to make window fittings waterproof, yet that is the issue. New cars commence life—usually—with windows and doors that keep rain out altogether, but gaskets and cement break down much too early in the game, and soon water is trickling into places it has no business entering. Within months your new car faces ruin. It purrs along magnificently, but unknown to you it is beginning to rust. Cars over two or three years of age begin to approach terminal rust damage around the entire bottom of the car—doors, fenders, trunks, and even gas tanks. It can all be arrested and reversed, even prevented. But nobody bothers.

That provides a golden opportunity to a wise buyer who is handy with antirust paint and a few simple tools and who knows where to look. The seller of the car won't point out rust damage to you, and if you don't know how to inspect for it, you won't find it.

Does this discussion mean that big cars have more rust than small? Since big cars have larger surfaces, there is more space for rust; so, the answer is a qualified yes. And more rust means more expense to repair the damage. Rust, however, is not partial to big cars. It occurs wherever water enters and remains, and small cars provide it with plenty of opportunities—in the same places.

Water enters in front, from windows and door gaskets, and even from radio antennas, as noted in the case of the early VW Rabbits, though those cars did not have a monopoly on this special defect.

Water from front window gaskets can ruin the components under the dash, and it also ruins the metal floor, to say nothing of the front carpet. The easiest way to repair such damage is to use a clear plastic sealer around the windshield—all around it. That is usually a slightly messy job, but it works. The best way is to remove the cosmetic metal around the windshield, if such exists, and replace any cement. But the gasket is what causes the leaks, and its replacement is a difficult job. It is best to use a dollop of water-resistant cement all around the gasket and try to avoid making a big mess in the process. If the car has the metal bezel around the windshield, you can pry it off and do the job, then replace it and remove any of the new cement that shows, using a solvent on it.

To prevent water from leaking in with the radio antenna on the fender, use the same tactic. However, there's a gasket through which the antenna enters the dash area on its way to the radio. That gasket is what leaks. Use cement on it.

Keeping water out of doors and lower panels around the car isn't nearly as easy. The panels below the trunk rust because water comes through the trunk gasket and/or through the rear window gasket. Rear window gaskets can be repaired and trunk gaskets can be replaced.

Panels below the doors rust out both from water coming

into the doors and not draining properly and from water leaking into the panel areas. Not all cars are alike in these matters, but a little investigation will enable you to learn the sources of the leaks.

Once you solve the problem of water entry, you are faced with the problem of repairing rust damage already there. That's a cram course in body repair and where gaping wounds are present, the easiest process is the use of body putty and backing material. That takes no talent—just the ability to follow directions and get the body putty correctly in place. You can rescue an entire fender that way, instead of paying $300 for a new one. (That price is not guaranteed.) Cost of body puttying? About $15. You still have to paint it, but you can buy spray cans for a few dollars that will give you fairly professional results. The beauty of it is that you develop skills as you go, and you can correct mistakes as you make them.

If you're serious about painting a car, you can beg, borrow, rent, or steal a compressor/sprayer and do the job in one day. Using a compressor/sprayer does not take talent; it takes only nerve or chutzpah. Always use enamel, not acrylic lacquer. Acrylic is what's on the car, unless it's one of several imports. It's much harder to use, especially for an amateur. (The compressor does need one thing; a twenty-watt plug.)

Inspecting for rust may be considered boorish by a seller— about like running your finger over the piano at a friend's house testing for dust. Don't be put off by any such analogies. A lot of rust can't be seen at all, and a lot of rust can cost $1,000 to repair. Pull up the front carpet. Usually you can pull it forward from the clutch/brake area or from under the seat. It's nailed down or otherwise anchored at the door. Some carpets are glued; you are stuck, there. However, if the glue is holding that's a good sign that the floor is free of rust and there are no leaks in front.

Examine the inside of the lower door, below the padding. Rust there isn't too serious, but make a note of it. Rust allowed to continue on the door at any point will eventually ruin it.

To find rust below the door requires that you bend over and look for it. Many people consider it undignified to bend

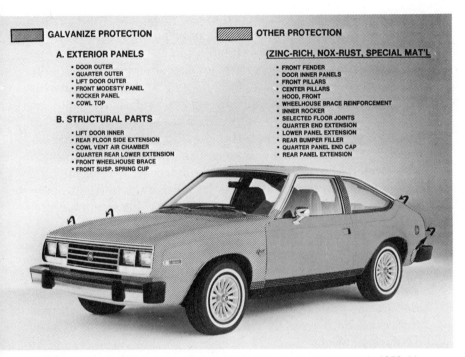

GALVANIZE PROTECTION

A. EXTERIOR PANELS

- DOOR OUTER
- QUARTER OUTER
- LIFT DOOR OUTER
- FRONT MODESTY PANEL
- ROCKER PANEL
- COWL TOP

B. STRUCTURAL PARTS

- LIFT DOOR INNER
- REAR FLOOR SIDE EXTENSION
- COWL VENT AIR CHAMBER
- QUARTER REAR LOWER EXTENSION
- FRONT WHEELHOUSE BRACE
- FRONT SUSP. SPRING CUP

OTHER PROTECTION

(ZINC-RICH, NOX-RUST, SPECIAL MAT'L

- FRONT FENDER
- DOOR INNER PANELS
- FRONT PILLARS
- CENTER PILLARS
- HOOD, FRONT
- WHEELHOUSE BRACE REINFORCEMENT
- INNER ROCKER
- SELECTED FLOOR JOINTS
- QUARTER END EXTENSION
- LOWER PANEL EXTENSION
- REAR BUMPER FILLER
- QUARTER PANEL END CAP
- REAR PANEL EXTENSION

FIGURE 12. One Detroit car maker has shown us how rust protection went in 1979. It's typical of most car manufacturers and is also an advance over earlier years, when special treatments weren't used.

over when buying some things but not others. A prized bottle of wine on a low shelf is an example of a bend-inducing purchase, and it is understandable that you might hesitate to make a similar move only to be rewarded by rust. But make the move; if you can avoid buying a car with rust below the doors, many moves are worth making.

Open the trunk and pull up the floor mat. Look for rust there and examine the insides of the fenders. They may be covered partly by cardboard or some other material. Pull it away, if it isn't glued or otherwise fastened. In any case, look below the car at these points—inside the fenders and below the trunk. Look also at the gas tank. Rust there can be terribly expensive, though you can fix a pinhole that leaks gas from a tank merely by using epoxy glue on it.

Looking for rust is looking for trouble, which is why

people don't like to do it, especially salesmen, who call rust "cancer." It isn't that at all if you know how to deal with it.

If you find rust on a car that interests you otherwise, you should consider that the professional cost of repairing a badly rusted fender or door is $200 to $300. And if one fender or door is badly rusted, you can expect to find it in others. Fenders may have inner linings that are supposed to prevent rust. Some do, some don't. But they do prevent you from examining the inside of the fender. If the rust has eaten through the fender, you will be able to see it easily, on the outside. Fender linings tend to cause rust to form at the bottoms of the fenders, because they trap water and soggy dirt at the bottom. Look there when examining any car with fender liners.

Major rust damage at any point in a car can cost up to $1,000. You can repair such damage yourself using body putty or fiberglass and cans of spray paint. The costs will be about $30 in materials plus a lot of your labor. Otherwise you should deduct the professional costs from the asking price, if the car interests you. Generally, dealer cars won't have a lot of rust. Beware all others.

In sum, rust damage can easily cost $1,000 to repair by a professional, and such damage can be overlooked by an unskilled, unwary buyer. Most of the worst rust is in places you don't see when you merely glance at a car. Examine a car for rust as carefully as you test-drive it or examine your bank balance.

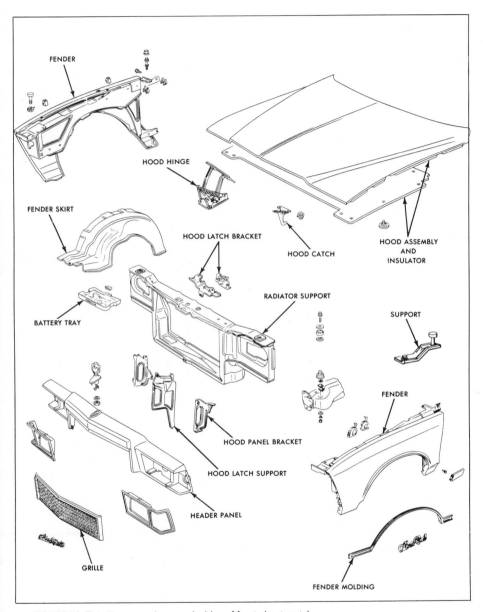

FENDER

HOOD HINGE

FENDER SKIRT

HOOD LATCH BRACKET

HOOD CATCH

HOOD ASSEMBLY
AND
INSULATOR

BATTERY TRAY

RADIATOR SUPPORT

SUPPORT

FENDER

HOOD PANEL BRACKET

HOOD LATCH SUPPORT

HEADER PANEL

GRILLE

FENDER MOLDING

FIGURE 13. This illustrates the complexities of front sheet metal.

II
THE WORLD
CAR MARKETS

8

Market Trends

THE WAR WITH IMPORTS

Buying an import versus buying a U.S. car is a distinction involving the national economy as well as the individual buyer. With imports taking half the California sales and close to a third of total sales in the U.S., and with automobile manufacturing in the U.S. coming apart at the seams, it behooves us to look carefully at cars and the car markets. Nobody expects imports to go away, but we don't want our automobile industry to go away either. What has the individual buyer to do with these questions?

Individuals are the basis of any free market; that is to say, individuals at the buying end of it. So each choice is a vote for the domestic industry or the import industry. Importing is a domestic industry, but it is a service industry with low labor components. Manufacturing automobiles is one of the backbone, labor-intensive industries. That may change, given robotics in a widening application. But robotics and the applications of it are far in the future. Now we don't even know what robots will do to employment.

Meanwhile, we have a backbone industry to worry about. It has been under a cloud since 1973. The individual buyer has voted against it in ever-increasing numbers. Why?

The big guzzler connotation was the main reason, once the oil embargo hit home. Allied to that was the carefully cultivated view in some circles (Nader, *Consumer Reports* magazine, and so on) that our cars were not as good. But now Detroit is putting out cars that match gas mileages of imports. Soon the whole U.S. auto industry will match the overseas auto industry in gas mileages.

Are U.S. cars as good? One count against them, perhaps, is their familiarity as against the exotic aura of the imports. The old, familiar Chevy and Plymouth have had to compete in a more open environment of marketing in which their comfortable, homely virtues were matched against the raciness of the imports. It must be admitted that some imports had avant-garde systems that warranted such interest and admiration. Austin, for example, brought over a front-drive minicar before it was even a gleam in the eye of the other big foreign manufacturers. And the VW bug, with its innovative engine and weird body design was an eye opener in more ways than one. Later on, the Japanese began their innovative ways, after securing their initial beachheads with plodding imitations of old Chevies and Plymouths. Subaru and others offered systems innovations beyond anything seen in Detroit—if you subtract Corvair, one of the world's most innovative cars. Also, Subaru offered more than innovation, as we note elsewhere. (So did Corvair: murder, according to Ralph Nader.)

In sports cars Detroit has always been a reluctant participant, knowing that they were involved in a market without mass appeal. Japan and Europe had no such qualms. They knew the value of getting sports car and buff magazines on their side. Detroit awoke too late to cash in on these markets, with their spillover impact on the mass car industry.

Now the newest Chevrolets are front-drive (excepting Chevette), rather avant-garde cars in a sense. The sense is that for the U.S. market the front-drive car remains somewhat experimental, despite the fact that General Motors has been making large front-drive cars for years: Toronado, and so on. Front drive doesn't quite feel like the rear-drive system. It steers differently, and because the engine and all the rest of the drive train are up there with the engine, instead of being spread back in a balancing act to the rear, the car simply behaves differently. It could not be otherwise. The sensation of being pulled forward, instead of being pushed, is the basic difference. But steering is slightly different also. And traction in snow and other difficult surfaces is incomparably better with front drive (or with the Porsche-Fiat-Corvair idea of putting everything in the rear). Front-drive cars are old hat in all other particulars.

Yet the imports did add strange devices and ways of manufacturing that had appeal. Subaru came up with a window-cranking system that is almost effortless, compared with the age-old, sluggish Detroit system that caused hair-tearing for decades. Did Detroit imitate it? You must be kidding. Detroit looks at Japan with poisoned darts, unfortunately.

Such common imports as Toyota, Datsun, and VW have become as familiar as the old Chevrolet. These cars had features worth imitation—for example, Toyota's neat valve lash adjustment. Mostly, Toyota and Datsun had a head start in the gas economy field. Their four-cylinder engines, though not a bit unusual at first, did one desirable, unusual thing: They economized on gas. Toyota and Datsun used tried and true engines placed in the usual in-line configuration. VW's Rabbit used a transverse engine (across the front and very daring). That stems from the fact that the usual Toyota and Datsun cars are rear drive, whereas Rabbit is front drive. But, as Heraclitus observed about 2,400 years ago, though not in reference to automobiles, "All is in flux." You can expect Toyota and Datsun front-drive cars in a flood—in far greater numbers than at present. At that point there won't be much difference between any engine and drive-train sequence you are likely to see.

Familiarity of Detroit products may or may not be a count

against them. But they are perceived to be less reliable, more likely to give you trouble than Japanese cars in particular. Also, U.S. car dealers are perceived to be a hardhearted, unreliable crew, whereas import dealers are somehow believed to be more solicitous of individual problems. One can adduce many testimonials to these propositions. Inevitably they are nothing more than anecdotes, heartrending perhaps but not conclusive. At any rate, when time and tide catch up with the imports and they become as familiar as the typical Detroit product, it is conceivable that they will come under similar clouds. Already the recall syndrome begins to affect imports. Toyota has rust problems. Honda not only has rust problems, but body rust also affects the suspension systems. U.S. car body rust has thus far been confined to fenders, rocker panels, and other nonframe, basic systems. Japanese innovation, in which rust has been extended to the very underpinnings of the vehicle, at least in the case of some Hondas (the Accord, about five or six years ago), will not cause the stock to go up.

Familiarity with European and Japanese cars will cause differences in our perception to disappear or to be minimized.

What differences are there? They may be slight but, as the French say about the differences between the sexes, they can be crucial. Engines differ in small ways. Toyota, for example, has a much better design for valve lash adjustment than VW has. Why better? The adjustments and the mechanical details for adjusting are much simpler, admit of easier accuracy, lower cost, and they last about as long. Because valve lash adjustment is important for engine performance, noise, and fuel efficiency, Toyota is way ahead of VW (and Omni/Horizon which use Rabbit engines, though not exclusively). To be sure, these adjustments need only be made every 25,000 miles or so. But it's something to think about.

On the other hand, Toyota had fender rust problems in some models in the late 1970s, not unlike the Chrysler-Plymouth problems of the same period, which resulted in recalls for Chrysler but not Toyota.

As we've already noted, front-drive cars are usually more expensive to repair because their drive train configurations are drastically different from those in rear-drive cars. If you shop for a front-drive car and discover a soupy clutch or transmission—one that lacks precision and smoothness—be aware that the costs of repair will be much greater than in a rear-drive car. Repairing a rear-drive clutch and/or transmission requires removing the long drive shaft to the rear wheels—relatively simple to do—to expose the gearbox. Clutch work requires removal of the gearbox and the clutch in that order. Again, it's a lot easier to do in the rear-drive car, hence less expensive. The front-drive transaxle is attached to the wheels. The clutch and transmission must deal not only with each other but also with the equivalent of the pinion gears that drive the wheels. Transaxles are far more complex, intertwined components than the separate clutch, transmission, and rear pinion gears in the rear-drive car.

Are front-drive cars too complex for their own good? Are they more likely to develop expensive defects more rapidly than the rear-drive cars? No. The transaxle, though more complicated, has developed into a fairly stable component. The gears, axles, and other devices wear about as well as the systems they have replaced. Hence any front-drive car that seems to have a transaxle in good condition should have about as good a life expectancy as the rear-drive car. Front-drive technology is very old, and despite the reluctance of Detroit to adopt it in small cars—because of the greater costs and complexities of it—the technology has matured. Early fragilities have been overcome. It will always be more expensive to repair, but the basic advantages will guarantee its dominance. Advantages are greater in cold climates with snow than in Florida or California. Traction on snow and ice is much more dependable. The space-saving, handling advantages operate everywhere.

Nevertheless, in the context of a discussion of greater repair costs, one should not overlook a used Chevette. There is no danger of an overlooked Chevette, since it leads all small cars in U.S. sales. But the Chevette has shown the attractions of automotive conservatism. The car is an old Chevy—front engine rear drive, with a standard, time-tested General Motors

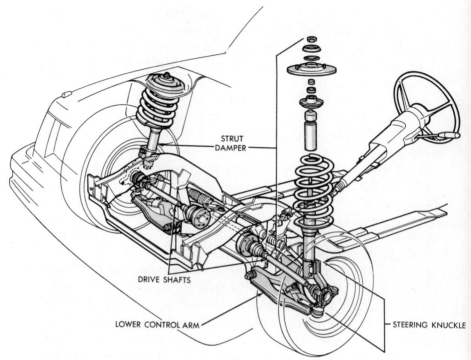

STRUT
DAMPER

DRIVE SHAFTS

LOWER CONTROL ARM

STEERING KNUCKLE

FIGURE 14. Front-drive suspension-steering system of a Dodge Omni, typical of such systems.

engine. It's the kind of car Datsun and Toyota copied back in the 1960s in preparation for their U.S. invasion. It worked then; it works now. Allowing for the electronic modernities in it, and the inevitable emission controls, the car isn't much different from cars you might have bought back in the 1960s, if you lived in Japan. (U.S. manufacturers scorned four-cylinder engines then, convinced that God intended cars to be driven by eight cylinders, and anyone who doubted it was an infidel at best.)

A Chevette shows the advantages of conservative designs; drive-train repairs are significantly lower than in a comparable front-drive configuration. Also, the car can compete in key areas with front-drive designs. Gas mileages are comparable, drivability and space are similar. Reliability is high. Reliability in a used car, it should be noted, depends on a book load of factors that we have been discussing, and Chevette has the same electronic features that diminish reliability in all other cars—ignition, for example. But mechanically the car is as good as any other. If this is not considered an unqualified endorsement, that is the nature of the beast—cars, new or used.

How long the Chevette will continue with its front-engine, rear-drive arrangement remains to be seen. Now that General Motors has gone heavily into front drive in both X-body and J-body cars, it is only a question of time until they use it in their smallest lines as well, for competitive if for no other reasons. That will be too bad; the Chevette is a great little car as it stands. But I would argue that the Vega also had its excellent points, which did not save it.

Along with Chevette in the rear-drive configuration for used-car considerations, the host of larger cars ("gas guzzlers") also enter for those who don't do a lot of driving or who want such a car for safety or other reasons. Reasons are not hard to find. Statistically, the 3,500–4,500-pound car is far safer than the minicar in an accident. It is also more coddling in its ways, with automatic transmission and all the power options and luxuries. Subcompacts and minicars are getting all the luxuries and needed power options, including brakes, steering, and so on. People who grew up with large cars often find the small ones difficult to take. The spaciousness of big cars, their softer, "boulevard" ride, their greater surge and power, appeal to some buying instincts, many of which were considered a rite of passage in Detroit advertising over the decades. Now that "small is better" has replaced the earlier opposite slogan, the lust for big cars may be abating. But sales figures continue to show interest in them, and if you only put a few thousand miles on them per year, you may conclude that they are the best buys of all.

Larger cars by the Detroit manufacturers are often available at low cost, and because they are no longer in the future plans of Detroit, they are becoming obsolete.

For smoothness of operation, the V-8 automatic-transmission product of Detroit is unbeatable, whether by Ford, Chrysler, or General Motors. There is little to choose among them; preferences are based on family indoctrination, advertising, and so forth.

CAR PRICING

Does it make any difference in price when you buy a car? Car prices are seasonal to some extent. When new ones are about to appear, there are discounts available on what is left over. Used cars fluctuate in price for many other reasons, chiefly their availability. In the past several years used cars have been expensive because of the great demand for them based on the high prices for new cars. So, as a general rule, when new cars don't sell, used cars do. That pushes up their price. Consider that a new Citation or Omni could cost $8,000 with desirable equipment. A three-year-old model would cost less than half that with the same equipment. If you found one with low mileage, which shouldn't be all that difficult, and would be willing to spend some labor doing rustproofing, you could get a car that would be almost as good as the new one. Admittedly, you would want to go over all the systems for the symptoms and possible replacements discussed in Part 1 before embarking on a 10,000-mile tour of the Canadian Rockies. But you now know how to go about it. All breakdown systems must be checked or renewed.

We have already noted that the quickest way to get a line on prices is to consult the local paper that has most car advertising. If you live in Cincinnati, it is no use to know what cars cost in San Francisco. The national price lists give you *average* costs of used cars, but you can judge that from local prices. Also, prices vary so much on cars of similar vintage, depending on equipment and condition as well as individual feeling about price, that merely reading about prices can be confusing. When you start to buy a used car, you may discover that the only useful way to go about it is to pick out the half dozen or so ads that interest you and simply go look at them, drive them, and talk about them with the owners or salesmen.

Reading about used cars—especially when it comes to price—can be terribly misleading.

The used-car market is divided many ways. Imports are both the lowest-priced and highest, whereas domestics are the biggest cars but not the smallest. A used Rolls Royce can cost over $50,000; a used Cadillac (supposedly the most luxurious domestic make) can cost as little as $1,000. No Rolls Royce, whatever its age and condition, can be bought for less than $5,000 or $10,000. Nowadays small cars tend to be more costly than large. A five-year-old VW Rabbit could cost $2,000 or $3,000, whereas a five-year-old U.S. car, such as a large Chrysler, would cost less than that. General Motors' small front-drive cars cost a lot more than the same vintage larger cars with rear drive. These conflicting tendencies in prices suggest that price movements in cars don't follow any particular patterns once you get past the several broad outlines we have noted.

If you decide to buy a used import, be prepared for a much greater variety of componentry than you have known from the familiar "big three" of Detroit, who have adapted each other's designs so persistently that they are more or less cloned imitations. To be sure, as car manufacturing becomes more internationalized, the differences between imports and domestics will diminish. We see this in the Omni-Horizon imitation of Rabbit, and we see it in such individual components as Holley carburetors, which are used in many cars around the world as well as in Detroit models. Also, brake designs are more or less identical; rack-and-pinion steering, strut suspension designs, and many internal engine components are interchangeable or very similar. This trend will continue. The differences are often in the way things are adjusted—as we noted in the case of valve lash adjustments in Toyota—or hung (installed), as in the configurations of exhaust systems, the components of which will be exactly or somewhat similar. All exhaust systems work alike, but measurements and configurations differ. From these differences others arise, including costs and installation difficulties.

Internationalization produces such things as a Mazda transaxle in the Ford Escort/Lynx as well as in the Mazda GLC. Mitsubishi's four-cylinder engines appear in Chrysler's Aries/Reliant K-cars as optional equipment, though Mitsubishi is setting up its own distribution network as of this writing for its own brand-name line of cars. Chrysler owns about 15 percent of the Japanese automaker, so it may continue to have access to engines (which are also identifiable as "silent shaft" engines in Mitsubishi lines). Renault, which owns American Motors as majority stockholder, distributes many of its own brand-name cars in the U.S. The famous Renault 5 is an especially appealing car, though early versions require a gasoline no longer available generally in the U.S.: premium leaded.

9

Imported Cars

THE LEADING IMPORTS

Volkswagen, the German giant manufacturer and rival of General Motors as a world manufacturer, produces cars in the U.S. under the Rabbit nameplate. Audi is also controlled by VW and has many related systems. The Rabbit may be described as a less costly version of the Audi, and when the Rabbit first appeared in 1974–75 it was described in somewhat less neutral terms when the comparison arose. However, VW Rabbits in recent years, as well as the various Audi models, have gone somewhat separate ways and have found their own markets. Audi produced the novel five-cylinder engine with other innovations. Audi also goes in for turbo-charging.

The Audi Fox, as far back as the 1974 model, has been recognized as a sterling example of German automotive finesse. Recognition goes back many decades, but for purposes of buying a used car I wouldn't recommend anything much earlier

FIGURE 15. VW manufactures the Rabbit and owns Audi and Porsche, three of the world's premier car lines. Porsche's 924 turbo engine, shown here, is an advanced design in a sports car. The three car lines are interrelated: Rabbit is the mass-market car, Porsche the sports car, and Audi the expensive sedan.

than 1974. Age has the same inevitable consequences on cars as it has on their drivers, and just as certain kinds of behavior in driving become reckless past certain ages and conditions, so too in buying. You may wish to buy earlier Audis for purposes of restoration; that is a subject for another book.

In such early Audis as the 1974 some endemic problems can occur. The Weber carburetors (by Holley) were often troublesome and hard to adjust. Low-mileage overhaul was a common prescription, one not unknown to Holleys in general. It may be admitted that carburetor overhaul can be caused by conditions existing before you get to the carburetor, specifically in the gas tank—for example, in early 1978 Omni/ Horizons—and in the lines and filters, especially when the filters appear separately and outside the carburetor. However, the Audi has a history of pleasing its audience, and it remains a generously proportioned, smoothly functioning luxury car. Six-year-old Audis can be found for under $2,000, and one sometimes finds them listed for less, with the intimidating "mechanic's special" tag affixed. To some people that is the best buy of all, given certain talents, time, and willingness, to say nothing of tools.

The Audi Fox was replaced by the Audi 4000 in 1979. It is slightly longer and wider, but otherwise it's similar. The Audi uses fuel injection, as does its cousin, the Rabbit.

Related to Audi incestuously is Porsche. These cars come from the same family and exchange some few systems and components. In Europe they are quite separate, but in the U.S. they are twins under the marketing banner of VW. In fact, the Porsche 924 uses a 121-cubic-inch engine that it gets from the VW truck division in Europe. Porsche is more expensive than Audi, with some models costing over $25,000 new. Porsche prices, like those of Audi, decline more slowly in the used-car market than most cars. However, that is a trait shared by most German cars, especially Mercedes-Benz.

Beginning in 1976, the Rabbit had fuel injection. Carburetors have declined in use in all VW and related lines, including Audi and Porsche. Remember that mechanical fuel injectors cause little more trouble and maintenance than carburetors, which is quite enough. But electronic fuel injection is a marvelously complex system that is computerized and hellishly expensive to repair. Some luxury cars have these systems and some don't. In theory the electronic part of the system should last forever, though the purely mechanical end results have the usual clogging and wearing problems common to all carburetion— the mixing and injecting of gas and air. You pay extra for them in the first place (when new) and continue to pay extra for them when they break down.

Audi prices, when new, start around $12,000 with minimum equipment. Used Audis are always in heavy demand. So they are expensive, but you can find them in good condition for around $3,000 and less than that if their condition is less and their age greater. The older the car, in the case of these expensive, luxury imports, the better the deal you can get if the car meets minimum standards of condition and drivability. That's because depreciation costs are far less in older cars. In buying such cars, pick out the most exclusive suburban dealer in your area and get acquainted with a salesman who will let you know when the right car comes along if you suggest that you are willing to pay his asking price. Even if that price is inflated by a couple of hundred dollars, it could be a great buy.

Some older Audis could have excessive rust and other problems; all cars have them as they age. But the point of buying an expensive car is that people tend to take better care of them, and rust care is one part of the deal. It's like any investment: The more you have in it, the more care you are likely to lavish on it. Expensive cars, when new, are considered an investment, because people who buy them consider everything they buy an investment. That is a key difference between people who have money and people who don't. It is investment sense, and it should be applied to used cars as well.

Audis, Porsches, and other luxury cars should be approached from that point of view, beginning with the right place to buy them.

The Audi 5000 Turbo is a front-drive sedan with the Audi five-cylinder engine. This car, when new, retails for over $18,000. It doesn't differ much from the Audi 4000 with the similar five-cylinder engine without turbocharging. Turbocharging is a system that gets extra power without burning extra gas. By tramping on the accelerator, you put the system into play. Its effect is similar to tramping on the accelerator of most cars that have a carburetor pump system designed to splash extra gas into the combustion process. Only the turbocharging doesn't take extra gas. The cars without it do.

Another German car in this price range is the BMW. Front engine, rear drive in configuration, it has several models beginning in price with the 320i, around $13,000 when new. Costlier models include the 528i and the 733i. These go up to about $33,000 when new. They are large luxury sedans, with poor gas mileage but great status and snob appeal. They obviously butt heads with Mercedes, and anyone interested in the one will be interested in the other. Mercedes sells far more of its cars than BMW in the U.S. But BMW is increasing its share of this luxury market.

A somewhat more interesting car, also in the luxury price

range, is the Saab. It has front drive. A sports sedan, it also has turbocharging. A smooth-as-silk power train is part of the attraction. Gas mileage isn't very good. Saab was once a fairly low-priced car, but as the dollar weakened in the late 1970s and Saab sales weren't euphoric, the company took a new tack: the luxury sports sedan. The car was based on the old power train, but the body was gussied up, and luxury additions pushed the price up. Needless to say, as the dollar strengthened, Saab did not lower prices. Prices of cars seem independent of currency fluctuations: They always go up. Dollar fluctuations, in other words, may cause imports to go up in price as the dollar goes down, but they do not cause the reverse when the dollar goes up. You have sticker shock in store if you haven't priced an import lately. To be sure, the standard, incontrovertible answer is that inflation makes prices go higher, no matter how the currency fluctuates. And that brings us back to square one: Used-car prices inflate much less than new-car prices, but they do inflate. And because labor is the big inflator, you can counter inflation if you are willing to spend your own labor in the renewing of the used car. What labor does to used cars is, in effect, to remanufacture them at the inflated rate.

The appeal of such cars as BMW, Mercedes, Saab, Volvo, and other sedans of this price range—$13,000 to $35,000 new—is better performance. These cars are more refined than Rabbit or Chevrolet engines. Their tolerances are closer, their designs use better materials, their efficiencies are higher for these and other reasons. It doesn't mean their breakdown systems are any more impervious to wear, and their gas mileages are usually less than lighter cars. Nothing can change that relationship—between weight and gas mileage—given similar engines. And all gas engines are similar, given the same number of cylinders, horsepower, and so on. Some cylinders may be arranged differently; combustion chambers may have different configurations; ignition systems differ slightly; and fuel systems differ markedly, as we've already stressed. But engines are engines if powered by gas. Diesels are an entirely different kettle of fish, which we discuss later.

People tend to keep these luxury sedans longer, so the

chances of buying a used BMW or whatever in a reasonable price range and with comparatively low mileage are usually good—at the right dealer. However, price declines are slower with these cars. In other words, depreciation isn't as rapid as with U.S. cars. So you find an eight-year-old Mercedes advertised for the price of a new, fully equipped Citation. In five years the Citation will have lost about three-fourths of its original cost, whereas the Mercedes probably would command a price not much lower than present asking price. (It would depend on condition and mileage in both cases.)

These high-priced luxury cars have one penalty not obvious: Maintenance and repair costs are considerably higher than for your Chevrolet or Plymouth. For one thing, most of the parts are imported. So you pay for an ocean voyage. This causes appreciation in their cost. It isn't necessary to comment on your appreciation of this fact.

In some cases foreign car dealers import mechanics. You also pay for their ocean voyage, to say nothing of the higher prices for their labor that goes with their status. It's like English butlers, who may not carry out the garbage more effectively in Houston but who are perceived to do so.

U.S. mechanics who are trained to repair the imports learn to do so quickly enough, but import car mechanics, even if American, continue to command higher wages in many places, especially if they specialize in cars of the rich—the very same cars I urge you to buy if you can.

We have been basically talking about the higher- and highest-priced imports. Their repair costs are higher in ordinary systems for reasons noted. It doesn't actually take more time to repair the MacPherson struts on an Italian luxury car than on a Citation, and the components may be identical. But usually the bill you receive will be greater. Many systems are not identical and higher costs result. The unfamiliar becomes the expensive. This is especially true in transmission and engine work. It is not true in body work, which is virtually the same for all cars—or should be. The repair of an Audi or Mercedes transmission could be much higher than a similar component in a Citation or Chevette. Again, the unfamiliar and the ocean-going addition to the job make the difference.

THE FRENCH CONNECTION

Renault's Le Car was supposed to compete with Toyota and Datsun in the mass subcompact market. It didn't, though it offered features not found on those cars. Mostly Renault had a marketing problem to overcome. But there were other problems. Early Le Cars had odd features that produced a poor image; the doors were hard to open because of an eccentric design, for example. But Le Car was called "typically French" in many of its features, including the softest ride of any small car. Note that the car is nineteen inches shorter than the Honda Civic, which isn't famed for its boulevard ride.

Le Car and other Renault models have been slow sellers in the U.S. Perhaps the American Motors connection will expand their market share. It will expand the number of dealers with parts and mechanics for them. One good aspect of Le Car has been its price, among the lowest front-drive cars in the U.S. Complaints have centered around such things as placement of controls, the cost and delay of repairs, and some early

FIGURE 16. Le Car's big rear door opens to 31.5 cubic feet of cargo space when the rear seat is folded down.

system breakdowns. Complaints like these are mostly subjective and anecdotal. It is hard to put a statistical face on
them. If you find a used Renault that runs well and pleases
you, forget the complaints. Just remember to trace through
our systems analysis procedures.

Larger Renaults include models 18 and 18i, which are
sports sedans to compete with Saab and other expensive
makes. But they cost less and so are interesting. The 18i is too
new to be found cluttering up many used-car lots, so any used
versions will be found primarily at AMC dealers or in the classified ads.

BRITISH CARS

British cars include the Jaguar and Rolls among luxury cars
and the now discontinued MG and MGB sports cars, as well as
the Triumph. Jaguar and Rolls are more or less handmade
cars, that is, they have more individual handmade finishing
than do other cars. It is both a mark of British backwardness in
car making and obstinacy about good works. The British have
been extraordinarily forward in car design, quality control,
prideful workmanship and care, and exactly opposite in the
backwardness of production efficiency and marketing savvy.
For reasons of this sort such cars as the MGB are highly
prized. That ill-fated car was made until 1980, so many MGBs
are available. They are cult cars, for good reasons. Their appearance alone has always marked them out; yet their prices
for sports cars were comparatively low. You can buy good used
MGBs for $3,000 to $8,000, depending on the year and the
equipment. Triumphs, with similar power trains, cost less.

The MGB convertible was highly prized. The top was
designed cannily for easy removal. In some models it also tore
because of unplanned stresses.

Power trains in these cars are interesting and a bit fussy.
Though the MG and MGB, as well as the Triumph models,
have a well-advertised appetite for parts, the fact is these cars
are rather elegantly designed. To be sure, their emission con-

trol systems are rather obstreperous and include such monstrosities as a "gulp valve," which costs about $35 and causes
backfiring when it gives up the ghost. I have already noted the
fuel pump in the rear trunk. Engine mounts work loose with
alarming ease (but there is no danger), and many gaskets may
need replacement—including the oil sump gasket, which
makes it necessary to raise the engine. Oil leaks are plentiful
and baffling. You can expect to buy a new water pump, gulp
valve, carburetor kit, and other engine parts prematurely.
Nevertheless, the engine has a beauty of performance, a quick
responsiveness and smoothness that you associate with much
more expensive machines. Both MGB and Triumph represent
sports car performance at low prices. The British have had a
bad press for their cars, but they rival the Japanese in quality
and style and surpass the Germans in problem solving. They
just don't get much credit. They command respect, hence are
the opposite of the famous comedian who gets no respect but
presumably can command a lot of credit.

What can one say about Rolls Royce and Jaguar? In a way
they are monstrosities. Rolls is mostly a hand-built car. What
else is made by hand today? Jaguar also has many hand-made
parts and fittings. These cars sop up too much petrol for our
purposes, but people who love them (and can afford them) will
have no other. They are an experience to drive. That cannot be
said for other expensive cars. BMW or Mercedes perform
smoothly and smartly, but so do a ton of other cars, including
Citation, which costs somewhat less. Jaguar and Rolls not only
perform smoothly, they also perform luxuriously. Perhaps that
is not something a car should do, but the British like to think
so, and millions of people around the world will continue to
believe it, even if British socialism triumphs and the proletarian car takes over. That would be Lada, a Russian-built Fiat
that I have not had the chance to drive, but press reports give
it good, sturdy marks. At present you can buy it in Canada. As
one who loves both the British and their cars, I can only lament
their passing (into another state of being—and manufacturing).

The prices of these cars—Jaguar, Rolls Royce—are such
that if you have to ask, you can't afford it. For one thing, few of

them are allowed to go to rack and ruin; when they deteriorate, they are renewed, no matter what is at issue. It is always a good bottom line thing to restore a Rolls or Jaguar. But if you can find one in the process of decay that is for sale at any reasonable price, and know something about restoration or know someone who does, the car is worth buying. Moreover, it is also worth keeping. Such cars appreciate, unlike your common Plymouth. Exotic cars have always been prized, but they have to be treated almost like family heirlooms. If a family of the 1930s, for example, had picked up an early Rolls for $100 or so (a fairly common possibility fifty years ago), it would be worth up to $100,000 today, restored. But closer to our age, a Packard is also a valuable heirloom, and there are plenty of fifties Packards floating around. These U.S. cars, if restored, are valuable and will also appreciate.

But let's get back to transportation. We're still talking imports.

We've been skimming off the cream—the mostly high priced luxury cars, at least the ones you are most likely to encounter. We've not talked about Volvo, Peugeot and Mazda, mostly because the numbers are small, at least as regards their affluent models. Mazda does send us their low-priced GLC, which we will discuss in the following section. And their sports car, RX-7 is interesting because it isn't terribly expensive, as these things go. But Peugeot and Volvo are expensive cars without unusual features. People who buy them generally like them, but the factor of maintenance and the rarity of dealers and mechanics all conspire against them. They could be the best cars in the world—which they are not—and yet cause hesitation in any buyer who considers such things as scarcity and cost of parts, the rarity of dealers, and the few mechanics who know the cars. However, if you live near a dealer and don't do much out-of-town driving, none of this will matter. One could say the same about the even more rarefied Citroen, Ferrari, Lamborghini, and others of that ilk. You won't find them on used car lots very often, unless you go to Italy or France, and even there you would pay a pretty price.

LOW-PRICED IMPORTS

Lower-priced imports begin with Datsun (now Nissan) and Toyota. These cars dominate the markets from overseas. Though their big sellers are among the lowest-priced new cars, they don't remain that way when they become used cars. This transformation, which usually accompanies big drops in price, doesn't quite have that effect with Datsun and Toyota. They retain much of their original price as they age. The reason is the usual: supply and demand.

Toyota and Datsun are the Japanese versions of General Motors and Ford, only it isn't clear which is which. They produce a full line of cars, though they have only recently sent front-drive cars to the U.S. Both companies have concentrated on fundamentals—economical, reliable, durable engines that are easy to maintain and repair; body integrity and generally boring, serviceable products. (When you consider the sensational innovation represented by Corvair from GM in the 1960s, comparing it with the stodgy Japanese and European cars that killed the Corvair, you can only sigh in wonder at a

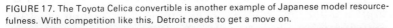

FIGURE 17. The Toyota Celica convertible is another example of Japanese model resourcefulness. With competition like this, Detroit needs to get a move on.

gullible public that bought the propaganda against Corvair, which came not only from Ralph Nader but also from deep inside General Motors.)

The least expensive cars by Toyota have been Toyota Corona, Corolla, and more recently the Starlet and the front-drive Tercel. The Tercel has the enviable distinction of being the lowest-priced front-drive car in the U.S. It's a good one, though not as good as the somewhat costlier Rabbit and its U.S. derivatives, Omni/Horizon.

THE SPORTS CAR

Toyota's Celica line is their sports car, with the more posh Celica Supra. Celica competes in cost with the $10,000-and-over (new price) sports car. One chooses these cars for appearance and what they do for the individual ego, so it is pointless to attempt to decide the "best buys" among them. However, the MGB can be bought for a lot less, and it's every bit as good.

Sports cars are not, however, entirely a matter of frivolity, as the preceding paragraph seems to imply. These cars respond to the driver's ego in rather different ways than the typical suburban vehicle. They enfold you in their cockpits, making you feel like the pilot of a B-52; their response to the road differs from your old Buick V-8 so much that you might be appalled by the enormous difference in road feel. Because spaces are smaller, with room for only two people and a small amount of baggage, the typical sound systems have been built up to terrifying levels of volume and fidelity. These aspects create an environment of living dangerously, especially when you add their low-slung height and tiny overall dimensions, which would enable a truck to run over you if you don't watch out. There is no intention to turn anyone off sports cars; on the contrary, they offer motoring charms of a different sort. It's like marching to a different drummer in other contexts, and only a stuffed shirt or totalitarian would object.

The question of which car to buy is not entirely resolved by noting the lower prices of the British cars, which are now obsolete and disappearing. Triumph and MG (or MGB) are the best buys in terms of price/performance, but what good is that if you can't find any?

So you look at the Japanese cars and Corvette. Corvette is also too expensive, but it is an interesting car. Mazda's RX-7 is at present the cult car among the aficionados. Because it has a rotary engine, now improved and less likely to blow a gasket, it is a high-performance car. The rotary engine can outperform a gas engine the same size and weight by a ton, but in the past it required a major engine overhaul at ridiculously low mileage. Current reports indicate that this problem has been overcome. Not overcome is poor gas mileages; the rotary engine has never been able to do much better than 17 or 18 miles per gallon. That may be enough in view of the other charms the car possesses.

A discussion of Corvette appears later.

One reason for the huge success of the Toyota-Datsun lines in the U.S. is their conservative design. These cars, as noted, started coming over here when they were not much more than copies of old Chevies, with a slight Japanese accent here and there. One thing they couldn't copy was the four-cylinder economical engine, which guaranteed their success early on and made the cars essential to our economy after the Arab oil embargo when we had no domestic versions. The

FIGURE 18. The Datsun 200-SX Hardtop SL, 1980 model, is a formidable contender for the sporty coupe dollar.

reason the Japanese couldn't copy them was because we had none to copy. American Motors had the Rambler, and there used to be four-cylinder engines from Detroit many years ago. Fortunately for them, the Japanese knew all this. But in 1973 U.S. cars were almost exclusively powered by the V-8 engine with automatic transmission. In a few years it is probable that you won't be able to find such an automobile. So, enjoy while you can; it was a great power train while it lasted. Meanwhile, the Japanese lead the world in four-cylinder engine developments, including their 35-mile-per-gallon gas engines (versus the 12-mile-per-gallon V-8).

European imports include the Fiat, Renault, VW, Leyland Motors (MG, etc.) among the more moderately priced lines, as well as the expensive cars we have already noted. Renault, like VW Rabbit, is becoming more Americanized, thanks to its American Motors connection.

Fiat is a popular lower-priced import. Fiat used front drive for a long time before it became mandatory in small cars. Many of its components are of standard international make, including Weber carburetors—which you find also in the VW Rabbit and many others—the kind of valve lash adjustments you find on the Rabbit that uses disks and dozens of other components. Front suspension systems have an ingenious simplicity that makes for easier overhaul and maintenance. Some of the models use a twin-overhead camshaft, which is a racer-type engine, or sports car engine, and some Fiats have odd places to house their engines—toward the rear, for example. Rear-engine cars are not unknown in the U.S. VW's bug and General Motors's Corvair used engines in the rear.

Fiat is a very big company with many different models, including the most innovative and the least, as far as engine placement and design are concerned. Cars such as the Fiat Spyder fall into the most innovative category, whereas other Fiats are standard, competitively designed and priced front drive or rear drive (engine in front). When you buy a Spyder, you get a sports car with a cult following. That makes for higher repair and maintenance costs. Ordinary Fiats are about average for repair costs, compared with other imports. Parts can be horrifyingly expensive, however.

FIGURE 19. Fiat X1/9 has an engine in the middle. It's an amazing little car, and considering that it is a sports car of enormous originality and verve, it isn't all that expensive.

THE RABBIT HABIT

VW's Rabbit is both German and American, and the U.S. version, made in Pennsylvania, is the one you will buy, unless you buy earlier models from 1975 to about 1978. The U.S. Rabbit is the same car as the Rabbit sold around the world, but it has a few touches aimed at American tastes—especially the cosmetics of it. The car today is one of the basic front-drive designs. Most owners like them, once you get past the rather steep initial price. After all, you can buy the Chrysler Omni/ Horizon for less money, and much of it comes from Rabbit.

Don't buy a '74 or '75 Rabbit unless you get one that has had a valve rebuilding job, a new fusebox with the fault corrected that caused the need for it, a new set of front wheel bearings, a carburetor overhaul, an air pump overhaul, an alternator overhaul, master cylinder rebuilding, a front brake overhaul (new pads at least), and a new accelerator chain link (from the gas pedal to the carburetor). Are there no exceptions to this draconian decree? Certainly. Test all the prescribed systems, as detailed earlier. For example, make sure that the brake lights work; if they don't that's a sign of fusebox rust, though it could be a lot simpler; merely burned out bulbs or the brake switch in the engine. If the carburetor is behaving, don't worry about it. Ditto the alternator. But be very picky about valves. Valve guides in early Rabbits wore out early in the game, causing premature oil burning. As for front wheel bearings, drive the car in an area without noise, open the windows, coast in neutral, then coast in high gear. Any gear noise should be tracked down. If there is noise in neutral, that almost certainly means wheel bearings—a costly job and one that must not be put off. Wheel bearings in any car must always be repaired at once, and in front-drive cars they are under added strain. Noise in high gear but not in neutral could be benign: normal wear and tear but not threatening.

Beginning in 1976–77, the Rabbit has improved, and later models were more improved, even though basic designs remained. Note that the 1975 model was the last in which carburetors were used almost entirely. Fuel injection began to take over in 1976.

Somebody might retort to my bill of particulars against Rabbit, that all I'm saying is, "Check out systems most likely to need replacement, which are no different from any other used car." Yes and no. Few cars need valve jobs at 35,000 to 50,000 miles. Most '75 and '76 Rabbits do, thanks to cheap metal in the valve train—the lifter housings. Front wheel bearings in these cars are terribly expensive to replace and too often need replacement at early mileages. It's partly the front-drive syndrome in which far more stress is placed on front bearings. U.S. cars with rear drive virtually never need front wheel bearing replacement if grease is applied every 15,000 miles. That might work also for Rabbit except that you can't grease them; they are "permanently greased." Permanence, in car parlance, is a "sometime thing" to quote "Porgy and Bess." The air pump, which not all Rabbits have, costs $256 to replace. That device can be greased, but nobody will do it, and it can only be done if you take it apart. There are no jets or provisions for greasing. But the job isn't all that difficult, whereas taking apart the front bearings requires expensive, specialized equipment and a lot of work. Even the Weber carburetors have highly questionable work habits. The accelerator pump and the choke pump tear far earlier than they should. However, I agree here that if the carburetor is working, the chances are that no further investigation is needed. One doesn't rebuild a carburetor on suspicion alone, though some paranoia is well taken in these matters.

I go on at length about Rabbit because it is now an American car and a world leader in its field. Used Rabbits are expensive, highly desirable and sought after. With what you now know you can get a much better deal.

Mazda's GLC and 626 are other cars that do well in the U.S. These are cars with conventional engines; beginning with the 1981 model the GLC is front drive. GLC is in the economy price class, a notch above Toyota Tercel in front-drive cars. GLC, when new, competes in price also with Omni/Horizon, a better car. In the used-car market its price would be similar. There is a tendency to view Japanese cars as something of a mechanical miracle. That is not the case, and the Mazda rotary engine is proof that Japanese designs can cause as many problems as the worst things to come out of Detroit. Indeed, Detroit has had no such major engine gaffe in modern history. Even the Vega was not charged with such drastic complaints and statistics of breakdown. The Pinto, for all the bad press it received, had a perfectly sound engine. Toyota's well-known rust problems, though not worse than anybody else's, are proof that no miracles exist in the automotive field.

Honda Civic and Honda Accord have carved out a spectacular career in the U.S. The Civic commenced its career in the U.S. as a snub-nosed ugly duckling that nonetheless won gas mileage awards. It was low in price, not too bad a car to drive, and wonderfully easy to park, given its size. It was also front drive. Accord is no longer in the low-priced field, if such a field exists. The Civic is also no longer an ugly duckling. It has been transformed into a svelte sedan, small though it may be. The car is a top choice for economy of operation. However, its maintenance and repair can be costly, and when you compare a car by Chevrolet, Ford, or Chrysler with similar features, you may be somewhat pained at the price of the Civic.

FIGURE 20. A Dodge Colt Wagon by Mitsubishi combines space and economy. It's a neat car to drive, too.

Cars by Mitsubishi—Colt and Champ—identical cars sold under the Dodge and Plymouth labels, belong in the low-priced field. Colt has had a fairly long history in the U.S. It's a lot like Datsun and Toyota, with rear drive until 1979, when it got front drive. It has not had the vogue of the Honda Civic, a more innovative car. But the older Colt with rear drive was as good as anything in its conservative class. More recently, Mitsubishi has come up with their "silent shaft" engine, which is supposed to improve performance, mileage, and durability. These things are hard to assess and the score is not in yet.

10

Domestic Cars

JAPAN VERSUS THE U.S.

Japan does many things right and virtually nothing wrong. The key to their success in cars is their ability to fill needs that go begging or unnoticed. Detroit couldn't believe oil shortages; the Japanese, who had no oil, believed it years ago. The four-cylinder car was scorned by Detroit: "Americans won't buy it." The Japanese understood economic factors better than Detroit; when pressed, Americans will save on transportation. The V-8 engine is not sacred; Detroit thought it was.

But when all is said and done, the ultimate calculation was political. We bowed before OPEC; Japan knew we would.

Anyone looking at Detroit (the code name for U.S. car manufacturing) who knew its golden days would be appalled at a once-proud industry that dominated the world. It is now on its knees. What ayatollah is responsible for the near death of this magnificent industrial colossus?

Arab oil. In 1973, before the Arab oil embargo, Japan had

only a tiny slice of the U.S. market. Detroit saw an ever-expanding market for its products. To be sure, the small Japanese and European cars were crowding Detroit models out of Europe and Japan. They had no oil, and even these places loved their big cars. Oil was about $2.50 a barrel, and what difference did it make if it went up a dollar or two, as the Arabs were constantly suggesting? Americans loved their V-8 engines and their automatic transmissions. It was inconceivable that the U.S. would allow any outside power to interfere with such holy writ as the V-8 with its automatic shifter. Automatic transmission, which subtracted two or three miles per gallon, was like a personal slave doing plantation duty at knee-bending times. The V-8 engine was a guarantee that you could get ahead of anyone who had less authority. Then came Watergate, a powerless president, an Arab-Israeli war (not started by Israel), and wham! The $2.50 barrel of oil went to $10. Once it was established that U.S. power would no longer act on behalf of its basic industrial progress as it always had in the past, the Arabs started their little club, OPEC, which proceeded to beat the industrial nations over the head with regular price increases. From $2.50 a barrel to $40, the price soared with no end in sight. It has "stabilized" in the middle $30-a-barrel range for the time being. Nobody knows how long before another crisis erupts. Meanwhile, the car industry was virtually destroyed over night. Nobody wanted the guzzlers; these once great cars were now scorned.

But you can still buy them. A 1975 Chrysler Newport can be bought for a song; derusted, repainted, made to shine like new, it performs with silky smoothness and power—at 11 miles per gallon.

If you drive it only a few times a week, the elegance, spaciousness, and luxury are hard to equal. You can look at prices on new land yachts—Cadillac Fleetwood—at $18,000, and consider the used alternative.

What should you pay for them? Not much is asked. You can buy plenty of mid- or late-70s guzzlers for $1,000 to $2,000. In some cases ("jalopy corner" ads) they go for less. Then you can assume that the car will need everything: power train renewed, body rebuilt, painted, and so on. That would be prohibitive if you had to hire it out, but for the home mechanic . . . (That creature can do $1,000 worth of body work for about $25 to $50 worth of materials and a lot of elbow grease.) If such a car needs both a rebuilt transmission and engine—a strong possibility—the costs of professional renovation would be prohibitive. The transmission would cost around $600, the engine twice that. You would still have the body to contend with and a new paint job. So we're talking about $2,800 worth of renovation. If you bought the car for a song, it might be worth doing. Don't forget the suspension system and brakes, the electrical system and carburetion. The prices I speak about don't include these systems, nor do they include battery and tires.

The ultimate cost could be $3,800.

Realistically, given the Chrysler we're talking about (or any similar Buick, Oldsmobile, Cadillac, LTD, and so on), what could you expect?

Suppose the car has about 80,000 miles on it. That means it would have had many systems renewed at least once. Shock absorbers on these cars don't last much past 30,000 miles; brakes, ditto. Tires depend on types and mileage. Exhaust systems last about 40,000 miles; if the one on the car isn't new, expect to buy a new one. Carburetors need overhauling about every 40,000 miles. The cars we're talking about would have had at least one such job. Suspension systems would have some worn links, possibly including the ball joints and control arms, various other joints in the front, and leaking oil seals in the rear. Universal joints in the drive train could be worn. These are all possibilities; all should be examined, as we've noted, systematically, in earlier parts of the book. But if none of these systems are defective, and rust damage is not hopeless, you must still contend with the big, expensive drive-train systems with their whopping price tags.

One other consideration remains, once you get past the question of low gas mileage and high costs of renovation; appearance. The mid-'70s guzzlers were handsome cars, especially the big Chryslers. Thus, there may be an antique

FIGURE 21. This 1975 Pontaic LeMans, if bought at the right price and in the right condition, could be great second-car transportation.

market for them in years ahead. If you buy one, renovate it, and drive it for a few years and can put it aside as a future investment, the chances are good that it will be worth far more than it costs today. That is speculation, like any investment. For the present, the big guzzler role has been reversed; it is a great second car. A person who drives only to work and has one of those offices not too distant from home, will find the '70s guzzler the best of all transportation in a time of increasingly shaky public conveyance. The four-cylinder gas sipper remains the norm for heavy driving.

Let us admit that the enterprise involving an older big car is a lot of work. It can only be undertaken profitably when the car has some of its major systems more or less intact. That means either the car has comparatively low mileage—say 50,000 to 70,000—or has had major systems renewed. It is important to know the history of such cars. Nowadays the law requires that the odometer tell the truth about mileage, but nobody has to reveal what work has been done on a car. That is why it is essential that you know how to assess the condition of the car yourself. Keep in mind that the mileages I suggest are not excessive for the typical V-8 guzzler of the 1970s. These cars, and earlier ones, too, could go on for 200,000 miles without major system breakdowns in the engine if proper maintenance had been followed (mostly oil and grease). Engine bearings, rings, pistons, valve train, crankshaft, and camshaft wear are normal and inevitable. In a V-8 the concept of normal wear can include 200,000 miles. Nothing I have said eliminates the possibility of a major engine breakdown at far less mileage, but that refers to the fact of metal fatigue. Nobody can deal with that prospect.

The '70s Lincolns, Mercurys, Buicks, Cadillacs, Chryslers, and others of that ilk were land yachts. Some day, when new energy forms arise, such cars will return, assuming that the human race maintains some transportation sanity, an assumption that modern politics renders questionable. The great ocean liners have almost disappeared for similar reasons of energy guzzling, but the factor of time also made them obsolete. Cars don't get obsolete for that reason; big airliners will never replace cars, since you can't take them to the grocery or to nearby towns. The guzzlers disappeared entirely because of Arab oil price gouging, a political act. Given new politics and new energy—both more or less inevitable—the guzzlers will return. They are incomparably better than their replacements, but it could take decades, and meanwhile the supply of them is running out. You would do well to keep one around; supply and demand equations will never run out. But these cars take a lot of keeping.

If you decide to go into the antique car business, you could easily be burned. Read the literature and don't take my word for it. You could invest a lot of money and get nothing in return if you do it foolishly. Basically what I am advocating is transportation, for short distances.

Note that many cars in today's showrooms don't do that much better with a gallon of gas. General Motors and Ford continue to sell big cars. Buick Electra, on a wheelbase of 118.9 inches, with an overall length of 221.3 inches, width of 75.9 and height of 55.6, is an old-fashioned guzzler. The engine is a V-6, for which extravagant economy claims are made. Don't believe it. The car's weight of over 3,800 pounds makes economy impossible. If you get 15 miles per gallon in the city you are lucky. The old Chrysler I'm talking about will do about two-thirds that mileage, and it's a more luxurious guzzler. The Buick Electra costs about $13,000 new; the '75 Chrysler I talk about (or Buick and so on) costs about $1,000, to which you add renovation.

On the subject of Buick, the Riviera is an interesting neoguzzler with front-drive power train, which it shares with Cadillac Eldorado and Oldsmobile Toronado. These cars have a 114-inch wheelbase and about 3,700 pounds to move around. Note that in the old days the wheelbase was between 118 and 124 inches, and the curb weight was as much as 4,600 pounds. The neoguzzlers have lost some weight and size.

They have not yet lost their V-8 engines, which are scaled down somewhat in heft so that their mileages remain above my old '70s Chrysler—mostly because of less weight, not less horsepower. However, the V-8 engines have seen the handwriting on the wall; they do not have many more years to go. One day your son will say, "Daddy, what's a V-8 engine?" and if you can point to one out in the garage under a tarpaulin, you could be as smart as your son.

Note that in the Cadillac Eldorado version of the trio (Riviera and Toronado) you get an unusual engine in recent cars that switches from eight to six to four cylinders. This legerdemain is designed to improve gas mileage by shutting off unused cylinders in the same way that you shut off unused rooms, hoping to save heat. It works about as well, which is to say hardly at all. It also does one thing that your heat-saving strategy omits; it can interfere with normal driving activities. There have been complaints about this engine misbehaving: not going up to eight cylinders or down to the lower numbers. The complaint is against the computer, which manages the change from one group to another, and because computers handle such complaints, you know the end result.

Cadillac is nothing if not innovative. The recent Cimarron takes as its car of departure the General Motors J-car, the new front-drive compact. You may be more familiar with it in its Cavalier and Pontiac J2000 family names. The fact is the Cimarron shares power trains with these cars, not price tags. It has many more luxuries and options. You can gussy up the lower-priced cars with similar options and luxuries, but you still won't have a Cadillac.

The last of the big guzzlers that continue to be made in Detroit are the Cadillac Fleetwood and DeVille, the Ford LTD and Mercury Marquis. Buick Electra and Oldsmobile 98 also come in here. Undoubtedly these cars are on their last legs; one hears that they will all be replaced with smaller, front-drive cars. Note that these cars are smaller than their predecessors and have mostly six-cylinder engines with much less power than in the past. But they remain big, heavy cars with rather poor gas mileages. Their prices have gone up astronomically, too. As used cars they are quite expensive. That is why I tout the older '70s guzzlers—if you can find the right one.

Chrysler Newport and New Yorker are advertised, but their availability is clouded. One hopes that they will always exist.

Mercury Marquis and LTD were close relatives in luxury. Marquis was designed in the lap of luxury; it did not have an economy bone in its body, whereas LTD tried to be slightly more democratic. The Marquis featured such things as leather seats, a steering wheel in leather with a ring horn that you squeezed, thus eliminating the unsightly, plebeian center horn button. You might have trouble getting it to honk, but what the hell. If you smashed into something that a timely honk would have avoided, it was a small price to pay for eliminating the horn button.

One step above the Marquis was the Lincoln Continental. Related to that car but different in ways difficult to describe, since all these cars had many identical mechanical systems, was the Mark IV, V, and so forth. The latter car was designed for the conspicuous display of wealth rather than transportation. It had carpeting, upholstery, lighting, and other amenities that one associates with a movie set or a luxury liner. To repair any part of it costs as much as an ordinary used car. For example, to replace a wheel cover could set you back about $150, when that sum still qualified as money.

The power train that all these cars had in common was a huge V-8 engine—there were two or three engines in graduated levels of power, with the least of them around 430 CID (cubic-inch displacement)—and an automatic transmission so smooth that you couldn't feel or hear it shift.

A water pump in these cars was almost as big as the entire engine of a Honda Civic or Subaru.

But there is one thing to say about these luxury land cruisers: The parts and systems were so heavy and bulky that they generally had a much longer life expectancy than you get in the present breed of car. They were not cursed with all the electronic controls, computers, and so on, that commenced in the late 1970s. So when you began a journey in a Marquis, you had every reasonable expectation of getting there.

The modern Marquis, Continental, and so on, though burning a lot less gas and taking up less room on the highway as well as weighing a lot less, cannot offer such assurances, opulence, ego stroking, and display. Many people will not regret the loss of some or all of these characteristics, but surely the loss of the security they offered on the highway is regrettable.

If you find a 1978 Marquis, Continental, or Mark V, you may well be stunned by the garishness of it all in the case of Mark V, or the opulence of Marquis and Continental. In their heyday these cars were not considered extravagant, since they grew up on gas that cost a third of today's price. But as the '70s wore on, these cars wore out their welcome, especially after 1973. So, the late '70s examples of the breed were on the decline. Plenty of them are around, and many of them are in good health, awaiting only the price of gas. With these cars you must be especially careful of rust. Rear fenders and trunks were likely candidates. But it can all be contained and rescued. Body putty will renew the worst rust hole. Engines in these cars could run forever. Engine peripherals, including the various pumps, appliances, and luxury accessories, were heavy-duty devices with pretty good life expectancy. Check them all out conscientiously. Replacements are costly.

GENERAL MOTORS INNOVATIONS

General Motors has always had a streak of innovation, as exemplified by Corvette, Corvair, Vega, and Seville. This assessment tends to be overwhelmed by the fact that GM sells more cars than other U.S. manufacturers combined, and most of the cars they sell are not terribly innovative. Whenever they make an innovative car, they get a black eye for their pains, yet they continue to try. Of the cars just listed, only Corvette and Seville continue, and Corvette is a subsidized car, made for prestige reasons. You can still buy plenty of Vegas, but the last Corvair dates from 1969, and only a few were made that year. If you can find one of them in running condition and can put it up for a few years, it should appreciate handsomely. Corvair lovers are an obstinate breed, with clubs and rallies. At this late date it would not be terribly easy to buy one for transportation. Too many things can go wrong with the car and too few people know anything about it. Parts would be scarce and expensive.

We have already talked about the Vega, which is a more recent story and very much alive on the car lots. Remember that it was heavily criticized in its heyday (mid '70s) for rust and an engine that didn't last. As for the rust, oddly enough the model that was most susceptible to rust damage was the most expensive: the deluxe station wagon with luggage rack. The bolts that held the rack to the roof allowed rain to enter, sending rust streaks all over the body of the car. But if you put a little sealant around the bolts, you could prevent most of the rust. As for the engine, it is aluminum, which doesn't wear as well as cast iron, as we noted earlier. However, its fragility has been exaggerated, like most claims against Detroit. So if you can find a Vega without major rust damage or with damage and a very low price tag—perfectly possible—that runs fairly well, you could still have a good used car, given your willingness to tackle the problems. On the other hand, plenty of Vegas are out there without rust damage or rust that has been overcome. Depending on price—and again, it should be low, say around

$500 to $600—it could be a great buy. After all, the price of the car that replaced it—Citation—starts around $6,500 or more.

Citation, if not precisely a masterpiece, is certainly a fine small car, especially since it has been around long enough to have overcome any lingering doubts. The car uses standard General Motors components, including an engine, ignition system, and so on, that have been tested for years. With the Chevette it has become the biggest-selling Chevrolet.

FIGURE 22. Chevrolet's Citation is a revolutionary car for Detroit, even though the rest of the world would find it merely interesting. It introduced front-drive to General Motors' low-priced field.

Citation's basic engine is a standard GM inline four-cylinder with overhead valves and valve train, a camshaft down below driven by a gear off the crankshaft. The V-6 is a new version of an old GM engine that also has stood the test of time. Two banks of cylinders, three each, in a V shape, drive the crankshaft, exactly as in the V-8 engine. In fact, the V-6 is exactly like a V-8 that has had two cylinders sliced off the rear of it. The GM V-6 engine has become the new workhorse of the GM lines, replacing the V-8. It combines great sturdiness with durability. There are no better engines in the world.

The V arrangement ensures long, trouble-free life because it can generate low-wearing, high-torque power production, as in the V-8. Anyone who grew up with V-8 engines, whether by GM, Ford, Chrysler, or American Motors, will not be surprised at these statements. Citation (and its brothers and sisters elsewhere in the GM line) is thus a combination of a venerable tradition with all the novelties of ignition, carburetion, emission controls, and front-drive technologies that have grown up in the past decade.

Citations on a used-car lot are not inexpensive. They have had an enormous success at the box office, and it shows up in the slow decline of pricing as they age. Any Citation, Phoenix (Pontiac), Omega (Oldsmobile), or Skylark (Buick) is one of the best used cars you can buy—if you get a good one at the proper price. The details of shopping to eliminate the bad ones are not different from any other front-drive cars we have discussed.

The new Cavalier, or GM J-Car as it is also called, by Chevrolet, is slightly smaller than the Citation but more expensive. We have gone full circle; small is not only better, it is more expensive. The car is a super little car, but at these prices it had better be, since it must compete with such posh imports

FIGURE 23. A Cavalier convertible. This is a trade show car by Chevrolet. It is called a "concept" car. Translated, that could mean nothing more than a designer's fever. It could also mean a real world-class car. Cavalier is the newest Chevrolet.

as Celica and Honda Accord. It can and does. Again, it uses time-tested, refined GM components—and why not? It is a refined version of the Citation, smaller but about as roomy.

Also from General Motors is the front-drive intermediate, 104.9-inch wheelbase derived from Citation (X-body). Sporting such names as Celebrity (Chevrolet), Ciera (Oldsmobile), and Century, these cars are somewhat more stylish versions of Citation and the other X-body cars. They use the same basic drive trains. They are slightly longer and roomier, but not much. Needless to say, they are also more expensive.

What this leads up to is that the best single buy in any recent General Motors car is Citation, period.

But what about Chevrolet Malibu and others? These larger rear-drive cars, with curb weights around 3,100 pounds, V-6 engines, and wheelbases of 108 inches, will not produce much in gas mileage. The key statistic is the poundage, and anything over 2,500 pounds won't do well on gas. Moreover, these rear-drive cars don't have roominess equivalent to front drives of similar size, or even smaller. These cars are being replaced by front-drive designs, causing their imminent obsolescence, as with a thousand other cars. That should make them cost a bit less. So you might look twice at them, keeping the total picture in view.

Any discussion of General Motors should probably go into great detail about each branch of the line, including Oldsmobile and Pontiac. However, we know from the famous lawsuit over the Oldsmobile "rocket" engine "routinely replaced" with a Chevrolet engine, that there is less here than meets the eye. In other words, the differences among these cars are largely cosmetic. Once in a great while a big difference arises: Corvair had no counterpart anywhere else in the lines, and you don't find the equivalent of the Cadillac Fleetwood among the Chevrolets. These were exceptions; nowadays the exceptions are hard to find. If you are interested in Buick Regal, for example, which has the V-6 engine and turbocharging and is called a "personal luxury car," the precise meaning of which has never been explained, you should also know that Chevrolet Monte Carlo is a similar car with turbocharging as an option. Pontiac's Grand Prix and Oldsmobile's Cutlass Supreme are virtually identical with these cars. When new, these cars sell in the $9,000-to-$12,000 range, depending on equipment and model; they vary from "plain" two-door coupes to luxury options that add costly touches. These touches are mechanical and cosmetic—interior and exterior gadgets and finishes, electrical devices and rugs. You can buy several thousand dollars worth of such goodies rapidly. But why buy a car like this without them? You know that you aren't buying economical transportation; it is pointless to buy such a car without piling up the luxuries. Some of them, such as air conditioning, are more than luxuries if you live in Texas. Many people consider car air conditioning essential in New York for that matter.

This group of GM cars will change into front drive in the near future, depending on the GM fortunes immediately ahead. It costs huge amounts of money to make such changes, and the present state of the economy could cause postponement. Thus a used car from the group might be interesting.

Pontiac has the same cars in other groups, including the J2000 and the Phoenix, the two front-drive cars, as well as the other lines of rear-drive cars. Prices would fall a few dollars below Oldsmobile and Buick, possibly.

Corvette by GM (Chevrolet) is a car that remains outside the Detroit mainstream. The car competed briefly back in the 1950s with Ford's Thunderbird, then a sports car also. Ford gave up the ghost early in the game, unwilling to pay the large subsidies entailed in the profitless "image" car. (Ford didn't get the picture; they should have charged it to advertising.)

Corvette has lost some of its ferocity, but it remains a cult car, despite the lower horsepower of its engines. It is also an expensive car, even by sports car standards. Used Corvettes never go out of fashion. Indeed, the older they are, the better they are, according to some enthusiasts. Recent Corvettes have all the latest electronic, computerized gimmickry so essential to modern buffery. (Note: I do not say buffoonery.) Corvette buffs, like the other sports car enthusiasts, discern unique values in their car. One can neither confirm nor refute

FIGURE 24. A 1979 Corvette has a 5.7-liter engine as standard and a new automatic transmission that some sports car lovers abhor.

such perceptions on the basis of the machinery itself. High sophistication is the characteristic of the new Corvette, especially as it affects the fuel system. Ah, the fuel system! It's always the fuel system that dangles in front of the designing engineer. Corvette's is now computerized with electronic control. Something called "cross-fire injection" is the Corvette electronic ignition system, to go with the new version of the old 350 V-8 GM faithful engine.

Corvette has four-wheel, self-adjusting disk brakes. Not many cars have rear disk brakes. It also has an unusual suspension system, though it is a rear drive power train. Automatic transmission is also part of the new Corvette. Corvette has an enormous range of creature comforts and splashy touches of decoration and display. The car is considered an act of love by fans.

FORD, THE RELUCTANT DRAGON

Ford and Lincoln/Mercury cars have been slower than GM and Chrysler to change to front drive. Their only front-drive car is the Ford Escort/Mercury Lynx. However the discontinued Fiesta is front drive, and many of them are around. That's a good car, and plenty of people like it better than Escort. You can find used Fiestas all over the place. They are worth looking at, driving, and buying at the right prices. They are two-door cars, with inadequate leg room in the rear, and as with all such cars the rear seat defies easy entrance and exit. If you need that, you must buy a four-door car.

Escort/Lynx competes head on with Citation, Omni/ Horizon, Tercel, and so on. Few people will conclude that it competes successfully, especially with Citation and Omni. Now it is available in four-door (actually five-door, as the rear opening type is now called). The first year of its life was not reason for optimism, so it is well to avoid the earliest used models. But beginning with the 1981–82 models there have been a number of improvements, and these are the models of choice. When new they sell for $6,000 to $7,000 and more, always depending on options. When used the prices should be in the $3,500-to-$4,800 range, again depending on options and also condition and mileage.

Ford's guzzlers are in Lincoln/Mercury as well as in such cars as Cougar, LTD, and Thunderbird. If you can afford the gas, these cars—relics of the 1970s—continue their luxurious ways. They were and are marvelous cars, with all the caveats about rust and systems wear and deterioration to worry about.

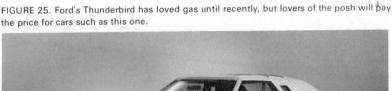

FIGURE 25. Ford's Thunderbird has loved gas until recently, but lovers of the posh will pay the price for cars such as this one.

One Ford product that is a bit curious is the Fairmont, a traditional car in rear-drive layout but modernized in recent years so that it obtains better gas mileage. If you continue to like rear-drive cars but deplore the guzzler's appetites, the Fairmont is for you. It gets mileages in the 20s and yet is adequately roomy. Fairmont is a modern car in that it has struts and rack-and-pinion steering—usually found in front-drive cars only. Other features include the lighter metals throughout to obtain better mileage without sacrificing roominess and strength. These are not entirely sales slogans. The car is a transition for the Ford Motor Company. It is a finger in the front-drive dike. But it works. It provides a modern feel in driving with required mileage, and it has the modern appearance—that is to say, boxy.

In weight, Fairmont is about 2,800 pounds, which is just shy of overweight. That means power steering is essential.

FIGURE 26. Ford's Fairmont has been a success story in gas mileage, in public acceptance, and in the fact that it allowed Ford to resist front-drive and yet turn out a competitive product.

In traditional Ford cars, Fairmont is the way to go. Pinto has had such a bad press that it may be found depressed in price. The tragic story of three girls burned to death in a Pinto dealt the car its death blow. Pinto gas tanks were no more vulnerable than any others of the period, and the car had some better stories to tell. The engine was a good one, though it had carburetion problems. Pinto's engine was, in fact, identical with Fairmont's and Mustang's. The engine was an inline, four-cylinder, 200-CID. It was neither the daintiest of sippers, nor was it in the guzzler class.

Other cars of the late 1970s, include the Mercury Capri, which is another Ford international auto, with a German-built engine by Ford. The Capri had MacPherson strut suspension, rack-and-pinion steering, and a 2,300-cubic-centimeter engine with an overhead camshaft. These rather advanced features for the rear-drive car gave Capri a vogue in the 1970s.

The Ford Granada (also Mercury Cougar) is one car in the 1980s much down-sized. It used to be a big intermediate, with 114-inch wheelbase and a gulping V-8 engine. Now it's a luxury compact, about like the GM X-body cars, but rear drive. Beginning with the 1983 models the car has a V-6 engine. It is actually a more expensive version of the Fairmont, whose four-cylinder engine it shared. But soon it will be doing its own thing, with the V-6, new for Ford, in these cars.

Depending on the economy and Ford's success, the plan is to make the Fairmont smaller and keep the Granada in the present size, with the larger engine. These are not changes for Granada, but any diminution in size of a corporate product requires huge expansion of costs—and ultimately of consumer prices. Cars are extremely costly to make smaller. It isn't like a steak, where smaller is cheaper.

CHRYSLER'S REPERTORY

When it comes to Chrysler, we are dealing with the big cars already discussed in detail. We also deal with Omni/Horizon, also discussed already at some length, and with the Aries/Reliant K-Cars.

Omni and Aries are related when both use the Chrysler four-cylinder engine. The relationship ends when Omni has the Rabbit engine or Reliant the Mitsubishi engine. The latter is more powerful than the Chrysler-built four-cylinder. It is too soon to declare one engine better than another, though we know about the Rabbit engine and its problems.

Chrysler's K-Car has been a big success, and deservedly

FIGURE 27. Omni/Horizon, Aries, and so on, by Chrysler, feature this interesting transaxle in the stick shift version. The transaxle replaces the transmission and differential with power output shafts. Note, these shafts have CV (constant velocity) joints to compensate for steering through the front power wheels.

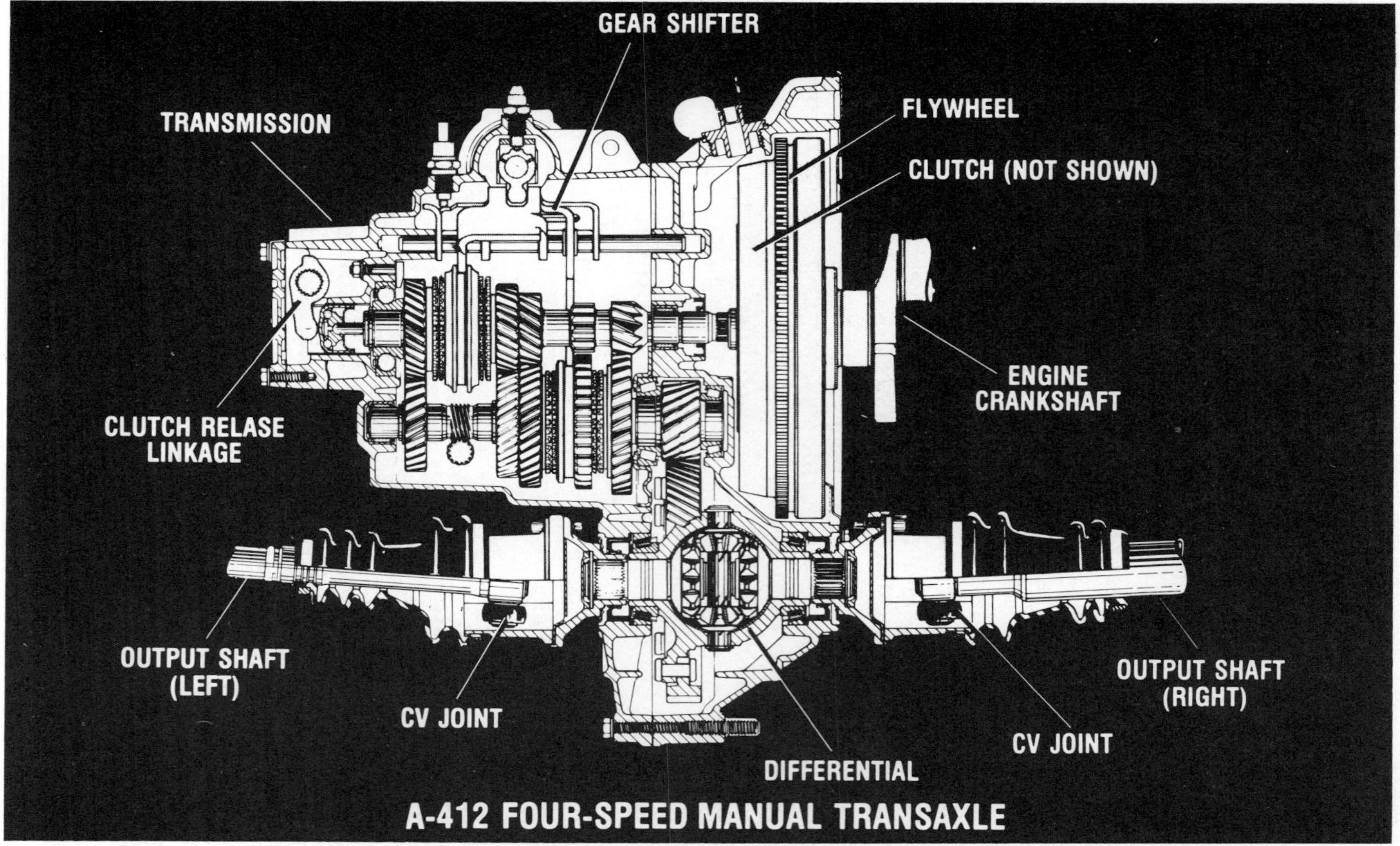

GEAR SHIFTER

FLYWHEEL

CLUTCH (NOT SHOWN)

ENGINE CRANKSHAFT

OUTPUT SHAFT (RIGHT)

CV JOINT

DIFFERENTIAL

CV JOINT

OUTPUT SHAFT (LEFT)

CLUTCH RELASE LINKAGE

TRANSMISSION

A-412 FOUR-SPEED MANUAL TRANSAXLE

so. In a better economic climate Chrysler would be well on the road to profitability and survival. The way things are, nothing is certain. As I write, the economy is sliding into recession, the depth of which nobody can predict, that being the nature of recessions, but Chrysler should survive based on its product. Chrysler has done enormously imaginative things, beginning with the Omni and now the K-Car. It may be a case of too much too late.

Used small Chrysler products have held up well in price. A three-year-old Omni with desirable options costs about $4,000. With reasonably low mileage it could be worth the dough, given the present price of new ones. The K-Car isn't much different in price when new, so its used prices should be similar. Both these cars are highly advanced, front-drive designs. When the same power trains are used—which they are in standard equipment—the basic differences are cosmetic. Optional engines change things. The new Chrysler four-cylinder engine is new, and its history cannot be foretold. Actually what was wrong with the Rabbit engine used in Omni/Horizon was not the engine but such peripherals as the fuel pump, which had nothing to do with VW.

One must remember, in dealing with Omni, Horizon, Reliant, and Aries, that these are computer-controlled engines. The computer is guaranteed, but nobody knows the life expectancy of these things. The computer and electronic ignition are instruments of the devil, but they cannot be avoided, since all cars made in the U.S. increasingly contain them. Some day, perhaps, the Tandem Computer Co. will sell Detroit its special backup computer idea, increasingly popular in big-business circles. The addition of an extra microprocessor whose sole function is to back up the first one may seem like conspicuous consumption to beleaguered car designers now locked in mortal combat with the Japanese and their eight-dollar-per-hour lower wage rate. Our designers might retort; "what will back up the backup computer?" after the old song "Who Takes Care of the Caretaker's Daughter When the Caretaker's Busy Taking Care?" Dereliction of duty can occur in any situation, human or otherwise. The odds rise in your favor when you add fail-safe devices, but they cause prices to rise.

Chrysler Corporation models from the mid and late 1970s include Plymouth Fury, Valiant, Duster, and Scamp; also Dodge Monaco, Coronet, Charger, and Dart. Dart and Valiant are twins; Monaco, Fury, and Chrysler are triplets. Charger was a "specialty car" of generous proportions, great power, and pizzazz, and a guzzler as well. Dart and Valiant were compact in size, with the Chrysler slant-six engine as the usual power. It was and is a great engine, durable, fairly economical for those times, with 11 to 15 miles per gallon. Any of these cars, bought at the right price and in the right condition, could be good second cars.

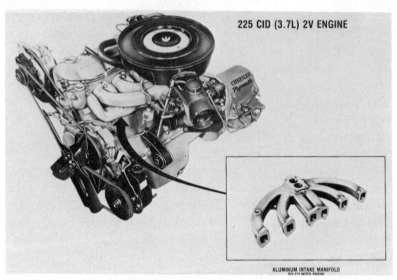

FIGURE 28. In 1978 the venerable, durable "slant six" engine by Chrysler was given an aluminum intake manifold to lighten its burdens. This engine was used throughout the Chrysler line for years.

AMERICAN MOTORS

American Motors once played a big role in U.S. car production. It had well over 5 percent of sales, and journalists referred to "the Big Four." American Motors now is owned by Renault, a big company indeed, but French and socialized.

When you drive a Jeep or a Concord, it doesn't necessarily make you a fellow traveler. Nothing is changed mechanically, and very little ideologically, once you get past the foreign ownership idea. In automobiles foreign ownership is not a very radical ideology. GM, Ford, Chrysler, Renault, VW, Fiat, Toyota, Mitsubishi, Datsun, and so on, all have interlocking ownership of auto manufacturing plants throughout the world. Fiat has the most unusual of all such deals; it operates in the USSR, where a Soviet version of Fiat is the biggest selling proletarian car. It is also exported under the name of Lada, as mentioned before.

American Motors and Renault hope to become a big presence in the U.S. once again, selling competitive front-drive cars. Le Car is their principal vehicle today. Meanwhile there is AMC Concord, a venerable car and a good one. Also, from the late 1970s, the Pacer may still be found. It looked like a spaceship when it came out, with its wraparound glass body. But it turned out to be the end of an era, not a beginning. With its old guzzling six-cylinder engine, its rather awkward interior, its weight and odd shape, it did little for AMC's solvency.

FIGURE 29. American Motors' Spirit Sedan is an offshoot of the Gremlin. Shown is the four-wheel drive system of the Eagle.

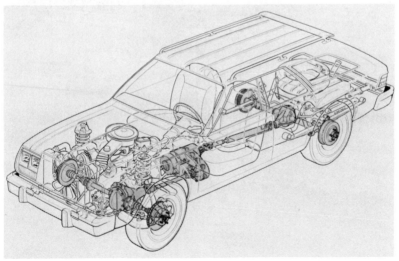

Today AMC is a company seeking a product, once past Jeep and Concord.

AMC's most recent product of note, aside from the merger with Renault, is the Eagle, a four-wheel-drive car. It is not a jeep or truck, it's a car. The only other car familiar to U.S. roads that has four-wheel drive is the Subaru. Eagle is larger, heavier, more powerful, with lower gas mileage. The first ones differ from the Subaru in that you couldn't get out of four-wheel drive, whereas Subaru is normally a two-wheel-drive until you shift into the four-wheel mode. Eagle, which looks like Concord, has a six-cylinder engine. AMC has devised a new transfer case to effect the turning of the four wheels under all conditions. Distribution of driving force (torque) requires that inevitable differences in rotating speeds between the drive shaft for the rear wheels and the drive shaft for the front, because of steering and turning requirements, be managed

FIGURE 30. The Eagle transfer case.

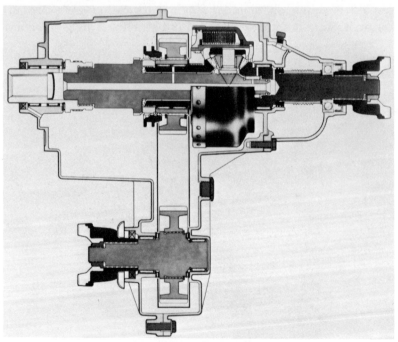

constantly and differently as speed changes and turning occurs. Something called a limited-slip, or slip-limiting, system is used, based on a new viscous coupling. The two shafts operate independently, in effect, since they don't have any mechanical lockup between them. Fluid coupling does the trick. Recent models enable you to shift in and out of four-wheel drive.

Eagle is of primary interest in states where traction is difficult at various times of the year, or in off-road driving. If you need such a car and can get by with less power, Subaru is probably a better buy. It turns into a regular Subaru, with high mileage, with a flick of the wrist. You can't do that with the early Eagle, but Eagle is capable of more work than Subaru and recent models let you use two-wheel traction.

11

Diesels

Diesel technology is standard in trucks and has been for years. It is more economical, and a big diesel engine has excellent durability and reliability. The keyword there is *big*. Engine compression in a diesel must be much higher than the 8-to-1 ratio common to gasoline engines because it takes much more pressure to ignite the fuel mix. No electrical firing occurs, as in a gas engine. The air is compressed in a ratio of about 22.5 to 1. At that rate air rises in temperature so rapidly that it is above the ignition point of the fuel. Hence the fuel can ignite without a spark. Compression is mostly of air in the diesel engine; it is only at the end of the compression cycle that the diesel fuel is injected into the combustion chamber. It ignites instantly. That drives the piston down and initiates the power cycle.

Diesel engines must have heavier, sturdier components; hence their use in trucks with big engine space. Also, diesel engines require a fuel injection system far more complex than even the electronic fuel systems in cars. That is because the metering and pressuring of the fuel, and its delivery at the correct timing to the compression chamber, makes extraordinary demands on both the delicacy and sturdiness of components as well as their adjustability. Diesel fuel injection systems have an extremely complicated task to perform. For one thing, in the gas engine the fuel mix is pulled in by engine vacuum. In the diesel there isn't any real fuel mix; fuel is injected into compressed air, the heat of which ignites the fuel. Fuel goes directly into the pressurized chamber instead of being combined with air in the carburetor, as with gas engines.

What this means for used-car buyers is that engines must be heavier and more complicated. Also, bigger engines require bigger peripheral components. For example, starting motors in large diesels are often driven by two big batteries.

Bigger engines add weight. That strains tires, bearings, brakes, and so on, unless they are weightier. Then the injection pump with its complications becomes "iffier" in a used diesel, according to Murphy's law. Also, it is not a do-it-yourself component, though it is a purely mechanical component; it is loaded with delicate devices: fasteners, valves, springs, and turning, pressurized chambers. To repair and adjust these components is highly specialized, unlike changing a tire or even overhauling a carburetor.

For these reasons, a used diesel car should not be looked at in the same light as a used gasoline engine car. It's a different animal. You can examine all the peripheral systems— the brakes, suspension, accessories, electrical and charging systems, cooling, and exhaust. If all check out okay, you can decide for yourself what your chances are with the engine and its injection pump. Mileage has a lot to do with it. If mileage is heavy, the injection pump will probably need overhaul. That's not an insuperable objection, since overhaul is not difficult for one accustomed to it. Therefore it isn't a prohibitively expensive job.

Diesel engines in trucks have great wear records, but outside the Mercedes diesel they are too new in U.S. markets to judge them for durability. The Rabbit diesel, the GM diesels, and the diesels coming from other places don't have enough data to be judged. The Mercedes diesel has an overall good record. It's a pretty expensive car.

Looked at objectively, there is no reason to expect an automobile diesel engine to be more durable than its gas counterpart. The same valves, pistons, gears, bearings, and so on, have similar or heavier wear. The fuel injection system is more complex than any comparable device on other engines. The fact that Mercedes diesels have long life doesn't mean others will follow. Mercedes cars often last longer. Whether that's because of the owners or the cars or the basic manufacturing isn't clear. Probably all three. The diesels you may expect to encounter in the used-car markets are mostly the GM, VW, and Mercedes-Benz. The Audi 5000 and VW Dasher diesels are too new to our shores for their appearance in the used-car markets.

When new the Rabbit diesel sells for around $9,000, the Mercedes between $18,000 and about $20,000. Audi lists new for close to $14,000. Dasher, which is more or less identical with VW, is slightly higher in cost. It has amenities lacking in Rabbit, just as with the gasoline Dasher.

In addition to the complexities and other drawbacks of diesels already noted, there are others that range from the annoying to the troubling. Diesel combustion has been linked to cancer, and even if the link is equipped with the usual modifying caveat that "it hasn't been established with certainty," it's clearly an avoidable risk.

The annoying aspects turn around starting. If you have trouble starting your gasoline engine, you are in for an even ruder awakening with diesel. Starting is accomplished with glow plugs that require about two minutes of waiting until they get ready to perform. Starting in very cold weather also requires that right viscosity of oil, without which the starting motor won't be able to turn the engine over adequately. Also, you must change oil more often and more scrupulously than with the gas engine. Difficult starting is further bolixed with terrible fumes and smoke because of imprecise combustion. The wrong fuel will congeal in temperatures below 20 or thereabouts and will stall the engine, ultimately stranding you. The very latest diesel engines have overcome a few of these problems (the 1979 models began to improve starting problems; advances continue to be made). But earlier cars will have delicate, questionable starting procedures—not exactly touch and go.

Diesels have sluggish performance habits and noisy engine responses to some accelerator pushes. You need unusual patience with these cars.

Complaints do not apply uniformly. Thus VW oil change is specified at 7,500 miles, not the 3,000 of most diesels. VW diesel is also a somewhat more nimble performer than the others. It should be noted that the main use of diesels is in bigger cars so that their space and luxury can be maintained along with better fuel mileages. So, the VW diesel is something of an anomaly. It also is a great fuel conserver, getting around 50 miles per gallon. Bigger diesels won't come close to that.

General Motors diesels include Oldsmobile and Cadillac. Other lines may get diesels. GM diesels start more reliably than any others, but there have been complaints about early breakdown of the fuel injection system. As noted, that's a

FIGURE 31. A 1978 General Motors diesel engine cutaway.

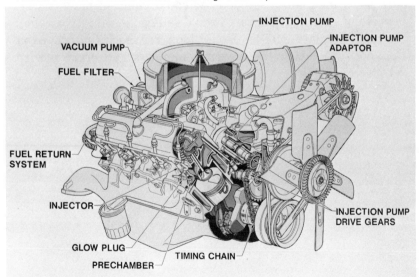

terribly complex, expensive component on which major surgery can mount up quickly into a $500 bill.

Mercedes diesel is king of the hill. It has been around longer than any other and its reliability quotient is higher than others, but so is its price. The car generally sells for about $5,000 more than the highest-priced GM diesel, the Cadillac Eldorado. It should be noted that you can get a number of Cadillac and Oldsmobile lines with diesel engines, all of them less expensive than Eldorado and most of them about half as expensive as Mercedes. Mercedes has earned its reputation. The only question, and one that is an individual matter, is has it also earned its high cost?

As a car to drive, the Mercedes is a better performer than the other big cars. It is closer to gas engine performance. That doesn't include starting. Glow plugs take their own sweet time, which is between one and two minutes.

One other diesel that might be encountered is the Peugeot 504. Anyone familiar with the gas engine version knows that this French car is an elegant luxury car with a few eccentricities but with mostly desirable habits of performance. The same is true of the diesel, and its price of around $10,000 when new means that a used car could come in much lower, especially now that diesels aren't selling as rapidly as they were in the late 1970s. Don't look for performance from Peugeot, other than its creature comforts and good service record.

BUYING
GUIDE

12
Dollar Considerations

PRICES AND INFLATION

New-car prices equal the price of a suburban home of not too many years ago. This suggests that the used car may have a new role: as an investment vehicle. You can buy a used car today—if you know how to buy—drive it for several years at minimum maintenance/repair costs, then recover virtually the entire purchase price. That means you have been paid to drive the car, figuring inflation at 10 percent annually, which is a recent average, no matter what it does in the future.

You cannot do that with a new car, which is priced so that the manufacturer and dealer recover the costs of inflation from the first purchaser. In addition, the new-car buyer pays for "depreciation" and shipping or travel costs. Depreciation is a catchall, subjective cost assessed by the manufacturer and dealer against the plummeting value of the new car once it leaves the showroom. Depreciation covers the costs of the disvalued public perception that attaches to any car not brand new. Shipping and delivery costs also have zoomed up recently. They are costs figured against all shipping related to the car, including the shipping of parts and components to the factory before assembly, as well as the finished car to the dealer. It's like paying for the cow's ride to the slaughterhouse when you buy the steak.

Hence the used-car buyer can avoid new-car depreciation costs, travel, and shipping as well as inflation.

Not all inflation costs are evaded, of course. But new-car costs have been inflated far more than those of used cars in recent years. The new car that cost $5,000 three years ago now costs $8,000 or thereabouts. This ratio of appreciation continues. But the two-year-old used car that cost $3,000 three years ago hasn't increased in price at all, or increased only a few dollars, and depreciation costs are way down; delivery costs are zero. Hence you are offered the possibility of obtaining a car that hasn't increased in price at all.

But, you may object, what about reliability, appearance, comfort, luxury, and all the other desiderata that cause people to go to showrooms like moths to flames?

That takes sophisticated used-car buying savvy—which is what you will learn from these pages—if you hope to salvage new-car qualities in your purchase. Knowledge may or may not be power, but it can be anti-inflationary.

Knowledge about costs can be based on "blue book" listings—official cost lists that, of course, are not binding on anyone. However, these published lists are useful guides. Local listings, which you find in the classified ads of newspapers, are the best guide, but you have to study them carefully over a period of time.

Expensive additions on new cars, such as air conditioning and deluxe stereo systems, power windows, power steering and brakes, and deluxe upholstery, are also expensive additions on used cars. Don't expect to buy a heavily equipped used car for the same price as a stripped-down version of the same car, unless other factors enter the picture—body rust, for example. That is why it is important to test these expensive things. Air conditioning that doesn't work is worth much less than a unit that does. Worn but deluxe upholstery is no bargain at any price.

Air conditioners cost about $600 when new. Expect to pay less than that on a used car, but not much. The same goes for other deluxe power goodies, such as steering and brakes, each of which costs over $100 new. Moreover, to repair malfunctioning expensive power equipment costs almost as much as the price of the original.

WHERE AND HOW TO BUY

Buying a car or any other expensive object involves considerations of budget, need, motivation, and other personal factors, as well as the problems of where, what, when, and how.

Perhaps it is well to consider the way car buying is approached nowadays. Young people "into" speed, show, machismo, and the various subtleties of group feeling about cars see a vehicle in terms of youthful status. Suburban housewives, if any remain, continue to view a car as a vital ingredient in successful workaday family life. Station wagons and sedans of high reliability are their first requirements. Women of every status are interested primarily in reliability because they are the most victimized by cars that fail on highways. Also, cars are supposed to be wholly beyond their understanding, despite the fact that many women have enrolled in car repair courses, where they routinely show better than or equal skills with men.

There is one group worth investigating even more carefully: the rich. People with money look at everything as an investment, in part. Cars bought by the rich fit that category. Such cars as Mercedes, Saab, Volvo, BMW, Lamborghini, Rolls Royce, Datsun Z cars, Cadillac, Audi, Jaguar, and so forth, are viewed by their buyers as investments—not only in status but also in financial terms. No car is an investment in the same way that the purchase of a Treasury bond, equity, or tax shelter plan returns money to the buyer. Cars don't pay dividends or rarely appreciate in selling value, but some cars depreciate less than others. The rich take better care of their cars because they can afford it, just as they take better (more expensive) care of everything they buy, as investment procedures. So, the wise used-car buyer who isn't rich should head for the dealers who specialize in cars of the rich. Such dealers are often found in suburbs. Therefore, go suburban. You may recall the Tom Lehrer song about the doctor who specialized in "diseases of the rich." A used-car buyer who specialized in cars of the rich may not do quite as well, but he does expose himself to the possibility of acquiring a car that had the right coddling. Coddled cars, when all the rhetoric is done, are still the best. Tender loving care, when applied to cars, has the same effect as it has on cats or dogs: They purr more readily, behave less churlishly (I know dogs don't purr). The trick is to find such a car.

BUYING EFFECTS

Buying anything affects people differently. Compulsive buyers have one set of procedures; cautious, frugal buyers have another. It is impossible and absurd to prescribe the same procedures for such differing impulses. However, both unite in the abstract idea of "getting the most for the money." The difference is that the one impulse is based as much on emotional need as it is on the practical need for a car, whereas the frugal person sees buying in terms of a practical need. There is little point in arguing Aesopian terms about these differences; they exist, nowhere more clearly than in the car market. If you buy from a friend, for example, you may make an enemy or nonfriend. If you go car hunting with the classified ads, bear in mind that a person selling a car through the ads is interested only in getting his price and cares nothing for you. Such a car could be a great bargain or fraud. The person selling the car won't tell you about his or her driving habits, will assure you that it was driven carefully, maintained scrupulously, and is the best car in the world. If you know about cars and can test it as we have prescribed, you can buy a great bargain, on occasion.

The new-car dealer, by contrast, knows a great deal about the car and would like to sell it to you, not to confuse, conceal, or cheat you, but rather to make you a customer. However, the price will usually be higher than anywhere else for comparable merchandise.

Compare the interests of the new-car dealer with those of the used-car dealer. At the car lot you buy from a selection of cars that have been bought at wholesale auctions, mostly on the basis of appearance, make, and model. The skein of transactions that makes these cars arrive at the lots does not allow for their care and feeding. Your lot car may be highly desirable in appearance, make, model, and even price, but it could be a mechanical disaster. Cars from the lots should be examined carefully.

One may break down used-car buying roughly into imports and domestic makes. To shop for an import it is best to visit a new-car dealer in U.S. cars, especially a surburban dealer. Such a dealer will have imports that have been traded in on a new U.S. car—in some cases. Dealers also get involved in the used-car auctions. But there is the possibility of getting an import car that hasn't been abused from such a situation.

If the asking price seems high, the first reaction should be that the car might be worth examining carefully. It might be worth the price, or something close to it. Don't be put off by an asking price that seems too high. You can always dicker, and if the price reflects the value of the car—as it might in the case of a reputable dealer—you are better off buying such a car. A used car with a high price could be the best buy of all. If you pay too much for a car that turns out to be a good one, you will forget the price soon enough, but you will never forget a bad car that was a bargain. The fact that a bad car seemed a bargain will not be remembered; the trauma of it could be disastrous.

13

The Great Recalls

Something needs to be said about the recalls of U.S. and foreign cars over the past decade. Recalls were initiated by the Department of Transportation. Detroit itself, prodded by the ever-present possibility of recalls, made them on its own. After a while, recalls became an unseen item on the sticker price. Today, as "sticker shock" has become a national disease, we should remind ourselves that part of the contributing cost comes from forcing Detroit to replace usually trivial parts in recall procedures. These are not warranty parts.

The whole system of recalls is a can of worms. Many recalls were absurd, involving trivial matters that came from a tiny segment of production, while vital defects went unnoticed over the entire production run. Detroit is partly to blame, the federal bureaucracy probably more to blame. The bureaucracy went looking for certain types of defects, which Detroit too willingly supplied. Quality control, if it had been better, would have eliminated most problems. It wasn't, and Detroit is to blame, but the bureaucracy was worse. It mandated such things as the seat belt that stalled the car or prevented it from starting unless it was correctly in place. That seat belt system was complex; it became part of an already too-complex system, the starting system. So naturally it interfered with starting and running. It does not take an engineering genius to predict such an outcome. There were several such systems, among them the early emission control systems.

Emission control has helped to clean up the air in big cities. It is essential. But the systems that were foisted on Detroit or devised by them ruined starting, idling, running, and so on. You can, of course, blame it all on OPEC. Oil price increases from $2.50 a barrel to $35 a barrel caused it all, but OPEC didn't cause our smog and air pollution, and if no OPEC existed, the air pollution would not be less. OPEC merely came along at a time when the U.S. government decided something had to be done about air, a realization considered much too tardy by people who like to breathe fresh air, a not insignificant part of the population. OPEC was merely a parallel menace. Unfortunately, both OPEC and air pollution continue their thriving careers.

Yet we have learned from both menaces; air pollution from cars can be controlled, and we could overcome OPEC. Neither prospect is in store because air pollution comes from many other sources, and OPEC shrewdly keeps the price of oil just below the point where it would become economically feasible to turn to alternative fuel sources. Apparently, we are too stupid, spineless, and incapacitated to bring new sources to market. Other countries are doing it, including the South Africans with coal gasification, Brazil with alcohol fuels, Europe with nuclear programs, and Israel with solar energy.

Auto emissions are now controlled adequately with many Rube Goldberg systems. The fact that there are many, after almost a decade of trying to cope with the problem, shows that we don't have a handle on it yet. All we have done is to make cars almost hopelessly complicated in the interests of slightly better air. These complications contribute to quality control

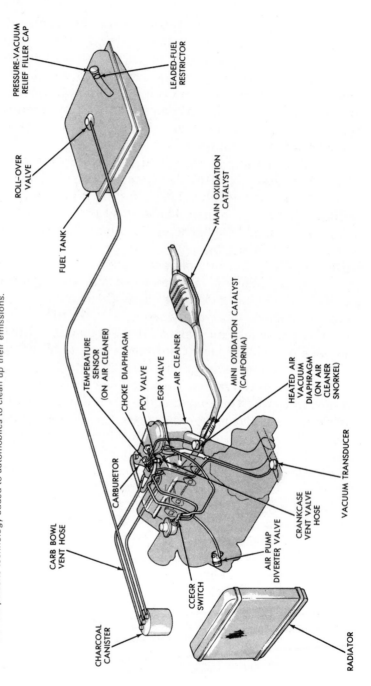

FIGURE 32. A Chrysler emission control system for Omni/Horizon, showing the major components—a whole new parasite technology added to automobiles to clean up their emissions.

problems, manufacturing problems, performance problems, and, in turn, they cause the recalls. Higher sticker prices complete the vicious cycle.

But don't the imports face the same problems? Yes and no. Consider that Chrysler products in the mid 1970s included fenders that rusted. Chrysler had to fix these fenders at a cost to them of hundreds of millions of dollars. Yet if one looks at other cars of the period, one sees that Toyota fenders also rusted and weren't recalled. What kind of suicide motivates our bureaucracy?

The fact is, neither Chrysler nor Toyota should have been recalled. Rusty fenders are as old as fenders. Some do, some don't; and it cannot be predicted in advance unless you are willing to spend intolerable sums on the rustproofing of fenders. Fenders rust primarily because moisture gets trapped in them. Avoiding moisture in fenders is like avoiding sin in people: It isn't likely to get done. Even when you add fender liners, as most Detroit products have done for years, you don't avoid fender rust. You can make it worse. Just as with sin, you can't make fender rust go away through bureaucratic legislation. You only make it worse. Fenders that rusted in the past were part of the owner's responsibility, once the car was bought, but rusty fenders pose no safety-related threat. When you make rust in fenders the responsibility of Detroit, not the owner, and through selective recalls force Detroit to take unusual steps, you force up the price of the product. That makes Detroit less competitive, and the whole dismal U.S. car story unravels, as it is doing presently.

Is this a plea for letting Detroit do its own thing? Detroit has no such option. It faces competition all over the world. Detroit is being forced, perhaps kicking and screaming, into a fully competitive posture. It will have to make products equal to Japan's and in many cases, it does. But the crazy patchwork of forced recalls, in which rusty fenders are recalled while serious, potentially disastrous defects are ignored, is equivalent to poisoning the atmosphere of auto production.

The whole, immense Detroit tragedy has many dimensions. Chrysler's financial predicament is one part of it, as is

Ford's unwillingness to assess the market correctly and General Motors' inability to price its product competitively. But the federal bureaucracy, throughout the 1970s, was not Detroit's little helper. It may have been its primary antagonist.

Finally, the U.S. consumer movement was one of the architects of the Detroit tragedy and remains so. The media continue to accord consumer spokesmen the highest profile and encouragement, though less hysterically than a decade ago, and such people know precisely how to gain maximum impact. It has been said that the antinuclear movement is partly responsible for OPEC's success and the U.S. industrial decline, but its success would not have been possible without a media willing to exploit it, a public willing to believe it, and nobody able to confront it or counter it. Meanwhile, the rest of the world that can afford it, is rushing in to fill the nuclear power vacuum we have created, because they see the interesting things nuclear energy does to a country's bottom-line energy costs.

What has consumerism to do with Detroit? Ralph Nader and critics of Detroit have convinced Americans that imports are better by implication. Detroit was caught by the 1973 oil embargo; the consumer movement capitalized on Detroit's dilemma, but automobile energy costs are related to all U.S. energy costs, and nuclear energy might have held down the rate of energy cost advance and even thwarted OPEC's most recent price moves, thus making the overall U.S. auto picture more competitive.

Detroit is not innocent in all this, but they are also not the perverse monsters they are made out to be. Their products are products of the times, including the times that permit U.S. labor rates to become almost double those of our chief competitor, Japan, and our labor productivity to drop. Is that Detroit's fault? Only partly. Labor negotiators have enjoyed a political clout in our society that enables this cost schedule to thrive for them. Detroit passed on to the consumer the added costs, including the costs of declining productivity that arose in part from the labor contracts—more vacations with pay, higher fringe benefits that had nothing to do with turning out cars, less use of automation than in Japan, and so on. All that added to inflation.

Japanese inflation has been far below the U.S. rate. Beginning in 1973, when the full force of OPEC commenced, inflation in the U.S. was substantially higher than in Japan. During the late 1970s our inflation rate rose as high as 18.5 percent, while that of Japan was always much lower, rarely going into double digits. Much the same can be said about West Germany, the other major source for our auto imports.

If our inflation rate constantly doubled that of Japan, it had to be reflected in relative costs of products made in the two countries, even allowing for currency adjustments. As price pressures increased from Japan, thanks to lower inflation and higher productivity there, Detroit grappled with cutting corners (quality control, for example), building factories outside the U.S. (where you might not get good labor situations and sources), and other last-ditch tactics.

So inflation was at the root of Detroit's problems, but in the fight against inflation now being waged, Detroit faces an even worse enemy: high interest rates. The high cost of borrowing plunged the economy into recession and stalled the sales of cars to levels Detroit hadn't suffered in twenty-five years.

So the federal bureaucracy remains one of the keys to Detroit's problems.

It should be noted, parenthetically, that if one culls the list of Toyota recalls, rusty fenders are conspicuous by their absence, but there are numerous recalls for fan belts that can break! This kind of bureaucratic madness must make the Japanese smile sardonically. To recall a car because of a possible belt rupture, no matter what kind of belt, is to say that cars should not be manufactured. Belts in cars are like wheels.

Nothing here should be interpreted as an argument for shoddy design and workmanship. Product recalls serve a useful function in our society. They do pick up dangerous tools and products that vary from the unhealthy to the poisonous. Also, automobile design and workmanship have declined in reliability dramatically over the past decade, caused mostly by the trauma of emission control mandates and Arab oil brinks-manship, which put Detroit into an accelerated program to make themselves over. Nobody likes to do that, least of all an industry that once led the world. The horrors of emission control regulations, high inflation, interest, recession, high unemployment, and the OPEC freedom to extort the industrial West made Detroit's proudest products no longer competitive with the Japanese and virtually destroyed the U.S. auto industry. We must understand the causes of some of the shoddy workmanship and designs, but we shóuld also under-stand that every car has almost as much as every other car's possibility for error. A car is a fragile thing, with present technology unable to offer much in the way of fail-safe designs and components. Anyone who admits this in the case of U.S. cars but thinks the imports don't exemplify it is ignorant or worse.

Auto recalls have gone on for many years now, with a life of their own. They are built into the system. Nobody knows precisely how or why they work. Mostly they impair the system, they raise sticker prices, they don't catch things that really need work, and they pick up things that seem preposterous. In 1974 and 1975 the Chrysler Newport was recalled for a lower control arm that could break away from the lower ball joint. Sure it could, if you took a sledge hammer to it, ran the car off a cliff, hit another Chrysler Newport head on at 35 to 70 miles an hour, and then ran it off a cliff. You have to wonder how these things get started. Finally one concludes that, as with Desdemona's reputation, they get started with falsely planted rumors. Deceit or somebody covering tracks must account for some of it. In normal driving and handling there is no way the Newport lower control arm can break at the ball joint.

Or consider another Chrysler car, the Dodge Omni. The big things wrong with it weren't cited at all by the bureaucracy, but a bunch of ridiculous claims were made, such as one against the control arm and ball joint system. Obviously, there is somebody running around who specializes in making absurd claims about Chrysler lower control arms who undoubtedly has a theory about them. In the real world these control arms never break or separate, or they do so only in wrecks or as a result of special driver abuse.

Most troubles with cars arise more often from inept mechanics than from bad designs. Car repair is complex and requires intelligence to master. People with that kind of mentality prefer to go into fields that pay better. So your chances of getting good repairs are slight. That's why I do all my own car repair work and urge everyone else to do the same. But there are degrees of difficulty, and car repair isn't as difficult as reading about it, so anyone who has gotten this far is already qualified to begin an engine tuneup and more.

14

American Car Prices

AMERICAN MOTORS

AMC's Gremlin, its chief claim to small-car fame, almost spanned the 1970s, beginning in 1970 and ending in 1978. It had a wheelbase of 96 inches, an overall length of 165.5 inches, with a curb weight of 2,700 to almost 3,000 pounds, depending on model and equipment. Gas mileage, with the usual six-cylinder, overhead valve engine and stick shift, was rarely above 15 MPG. Rabbit and Audi engines were used in 1977–78 in an attempt to compete with import car mileages. It failed; the car weighed too much, with the result that it had the worst of two worlds, an underpowered engine, an overweight body. The body design was poor in most ways, apart from its sawed-off appearance; it had no rear-seat leg room to speak of, measuring 27.8 inches, which is about 5 inches less than comfort requires.

Gremlin prices range all over the lot. A 1974 Gremlin lists for between $800 and $1,350, but, in the real world, the prices should be less. Thus, the dealer cost of a 1975 Gremlin two-door sedan was $2,479, which would have retailed for less than $3,000. You could find plenty of 1975 Gremlins for less than half that price today. Today's book prices on 1978 Gremlins—the last ones produced—are between $2,500 and $3,600, but, again, you can find them for a lot less. A Gremlin in good condition is a good buy at a low price. Despite poor mileage and no room in the rear, the power trains were good. So, if you don't need the rear seat, Gremlin is a good buy, albeit qualified heavily.

The AMC Hornet, which replaced the Rambler in a way and was itself replaced by the Concord, used the same power trains as the Rambler, with several exceptions, including two V-8 engines in several models. These were hardly improvements, and the last V-8 was used in 1977. Prices would be the same as or less than the Gremlin. The body is a conventional design and offers adequate space for rear passengers. So it is a far more useful car.

AMC's Concord is similar enough to the Hornet in size, with a wheelbase of 108 inches, overall length of 186, and the same curb weights, as if to perpetuate that car's merits and demerits. Price ranges of the most recent Concords were in the low-priced field, from $5,000 to $6,500. Prices of three-year-old Concords would be between $2,500 and $3,500. The best engine to buy would be the six-cylinder, 232 c.i.d. with 90 horsepower, available in '78 and '79 models. However, the most economical engine would be the four-cylinder 1980 engine, which is rated at 21 MPG. The 1980 car would cost $1,000 less than new car prices if bought in 1981, $1,500 less if bought in 1982, and so on. (Subtract about $500 a year.)

Eagle is a four-wheel-drive Concord. The 1980 Eagle would cost $1,000 less than the 1981. Eagle is in the $6,000-to-$7,000 range when new, depending on equipment. Any new car can cost $8,000 quickly. The history of AMC used cars is that they depreciate more than the competition. So used AMC cars can be excellent buys.

Pacer, which lived from 1975 to 1980, can be bought for very low prices. An unloved car, it was innovative in design,

FIGURE 33. American Motors' Eagle is a four-wheel-drive version of the Concord.

but the engine was the standard AMC six-cylinder (two of them) or an eight in the 1978–80 models. The small six offered over 15 MPG. Prices should be less than Concord or Gremlin, though similar. A 1975 could be as low as $600 or as high as $1,700.

Spirit replaced Gremlin. Though it looks different, it isn't. It has the same wheelbase, length, weight, terrible rear-seat leg room, and engines. Unless you buy the bigger engines, it lacks spirit. Then it lacks mileage. Prices would be at the low end of the scale for two- or three-year-old cars that commenced life selling in the $5,000-to-$6,500 range.

FIGURE 34. The Pacer enjoyed a brilliant body design, but it failed to sell.

CHRYSLER

Every family's happiness may be the same, according to Tolstoy, but every corporation's problems differ. Chrysler has the right products and a shrinking market, no cash flow, creditors with a shotgun after it, and interest rates with which it cannot cope. Chrysler faces doom unless something happens along all its problem fronts. It is an irony that of all the world's automakers the one that was in the forefront of adapting to the car environment looks like the first to fail. Chrysler was first in the U.S. with small, front-drive cars, facing up to General Motors, saying no. Remember that GM has always dictated policy in Detroit, and to disagree with GM in the Detroit scheme is to disagree with the president in the White House, or Brezhnev in the Kremlin. Safety dictates otherwise. But just as hanging powerfully concentrates a man's thoughts, so bottom-line red ink tends to make a corporation look beyond tradition. Chrysler certainly did that. Will it have to wait for heaven in order to be rewarded?

Part of the answer to that question depends on car buyers. Unless the word can be gotten out that Chrysler cars are no longer the big guzzlers of yore but are the canniest of small cars, and fully competitive with the Japanese and the Europeans, Chrysler is doomed. That would be both unjust and suicidal for U.S. industry, economy, the city of Detroit, and so on down the line.

Chrysler has done a sensational job of stretching one basic car into the semblance of a full line. Cordoba, between 1975 and 1979, was similar to the Dodge Charger, hence a "personal luxury" car. When personal luxuries disappeared in 1979, with the first of our most recent recessions, Cordoba followed. In its place there arose a less luxurious Cordoba. Cordoba, the first, had a wheelbase of 114.9 inches, hefty V-8 engines, from a 135 horsepower to a 235, and an overall length of 215.8 inches. Its curb weight was around 3,800 pounds. Expect to pay between $1,000 and $1,900 for 1975 Cordobas, depending on you know what. As you get closer to the present, add $500 at least to each year's model. If the car has deluxe equipment, you could double that amount, and if the mileage is low and the car is "clean," there is no telling what the asking price might be. Nobody knows exactly what a "clean" used car is since nobody has advertised a dirty one, so we have no basis for the comparisons necessary to define these things. Cordoba prices are as follows:

Year	Prices
1976	$1,200–$2,400
1977	$2,000–$3,000
1978	$2,500–$3,500
1979	$3,500–$4,500

FIGURE 35. Chrysler's Cordoba keeps changing its spots. This Cordoba is a hefty V-8 luxury car à la 1979. Today, it is a front-drive luxury car, much lighter and more economical.

Cordoba 1980 is shorter and lighter. It's a similar car to LeBaron and Dodge Diplomat. Wheelbase is now 112.7 inches, length is 210.1 inches. Weight is down to about 3,450 pounds. The engine selection ranges from the familiar Chrysler "slant six" to three V-8 engines, ranging in horsepower from 135 to 185. When you add horses, you add thirst. Prices for the 1980 used Cordoba now list at from $4,000 to $6,000.

Cordoba has had a splashy career, now ended. It has been replaced by the LeBaron. Keeping track of these disappearing cars is like following old vessels in the Sargasso Sea; they disappear without a trace, or the nameplates remain and the cars disappear. LeBaron commenced life in 1977 as a Dodge Aspen with the Plymouth Volare similar. A luxury version.

Prices for the first LeBarons are about $2,000 to $3,200 for the 1977. You add $500 to $1,000 to the 1978, and $1,000 to $1,500 for the 1979. 1980 prices are between $4,000 and $5,800. When 1981 prices are posted, they will reflect not only the new car prices they are based on but also the fact that the car is itself new—a front-drive Reliant/Aries sister. (It is more alluring than Reliant/Aries; so we arbitrarily say it is female.)

Engines are the slant six and several V-8s. Gas mileages, according to the EPA, were pretty good, ranging between 14.2 and 18.4 MPG. These first LeBarons were on a wheelbase of 112.7, which is larger in the case of the coupe than the Aspen/Volare they copied in other matters, but the same as the four-door sedan. The sedan weighs about 3,400, as with Cordoba. The two V-8s have 135 and 155 horsepower. Guess which one gets the better mileage.

Most recently, LeBaron is a "spinoff" of Reliant/Aries. Prices on used versions will be somewhat higher than these cars, because LeBaron remains a luxury version.

Thus as nameplates remain, while the cars they refer to become different animals, the LeBaron you look at will be (1) a compact-size mini-guzzler, designed to save gas and materials but not very good at it, and (2) the front-drive economy power train based on the latest Chrysler designs. To sort out price ranges on the latest car with the LeBaron nameplate, keep it in mind that age and condition remain the dominating factors. Then, any front-drive car will cost more than a comparable rear drive, whereas luxury options cost whatever they did when new minus whatever dollars you can get the seller to deduct. Not many is the rule.

Chrysler Imperial died in 1973, so any price lists will be in the nature of a requiem. On a wheelbase of 127 inches, with a curb weight of more than 5,000 pounds, Imperial lived up to its name. It is now in terribly short supply. Prices should be between $300 and $1,200.

Chrysler Newport and New Yorker, which have gone through various metamorphoses of size, horsepower, and systems designs, in the last decade, culminated in a car that wasn't a Chrysler. It was a Dodge (Monaco) or Plymouth (Fury). Okay, the wheelbase of 124 inches shrank to 118.5, the length lost 4 inches, the weight 800 pounds—from 4,400 to 3,600. However, smaller being better, the final Newports were good cars well worth keeping and driving as a second car. Prices of mid-1970s Newports should be between $800 and $2,000. Prices of the 1977–78 vary between $1,800 and $4,000. A "mechanic's special" would be less. The 1979–80 smaller Newports will cost more. Figure them between $3,000 and $7,400. The last roundup of the big Chryslers found them with the largest engine at 195 horsepower V-8 (360-CID), the smallest the 110 horsepower, 225-CID slant six.

The same forces—namely the U.S. government and competition—that made Chrysler a small-car, front-drive corporation, had identical results at Dodge and Plymouth. Chrysler's agreement with the feds that bailed them out also nailed them down; namely, they had to abandon the "full line" status and become a small-car manufacturer. That has happened rapidly. Every car now on the active list is a variant of the basic Omni/Horizon. It is true of Reliant/Aries and any other nameplate from Chrysler/Dodge/Plymouth excepting Newport/ New Yorker. Before the fall things were different, not necessarily better.

Dodge's Aspen replaced the compact Dart in 1976. Dart had been a good seller from 1971 to 1976, featuring high mileage for the period from the slant-six engine, and not-so-high from the bigger engines, including three V-8s. Dart and Hornet locked horns on gas mileage in those days, but only with the smallest engines, when you could do up to 18.6 MPG, according to the EPA. Dart prices in the mid-1970s models are between $800 and $2,500, all things considered. Thus you could pay up to $2,500 for a 1976 Dart with everything on it, all in good condition, according to the official price lists. If you could find such a car, it would, of course, be well worth it.

The Aspen replacement continued the same engine

repertory but slightly decreased EPA mileages. This was hardly a stirring response to the problems of the times, but neither was the EPA, according to Chrysler and Detroit.

Aspen prices continue those of Dart, and an Aspen between 1977 and 1980 would go from $1,600 up to $4,600. Thus the official lists are:

Year	Prices
1977	$1,600–$3,000
1978	$2,400–$3,575
1979	$2,750–$4,100
1980	$3,500–$4,600

We stress these are national prices; they have little to do with the local numbers and less than that to do with individual cars.

Dodge Challenger and Charger were cars that flourished until 1974. They were big, burly, razzmatazz cars, with special appeal to the young. Outfitted with the biggest Chrysler engines (425 horsepower), they burned gas at the rate of 7.1 miles per gallon, a statistic for gleeful contemplation at an OPEC meeting but not reassuring elsewhere. So Challenger and Charger went the way of all flesh. They were not exactly the same cars. Challenger was all flash, built on a 110-inch wheelbase, with a body weight of about 3,200 pounds. Charger was on a 115-inch wheelbase, with a body weight of about 3,450 pounds. It was called a "muscle car" in those days. No translation of that term is operative today. Prices of these cars are similar, but prices of most U.S. cars on the lots resemble each other when you compare cars of the same years and equipment.

Challenger and Charger died in 1974. One cannot recommend these cars at this late date, though the 1974 Challenger with the slant-six 125-horsepower engine was a good economy car, and so was the Charger. Challenger was rated at 19.4 MPG with the smallest engine; we have cited the mileage with the biggest engine. The fact that there is such a huge disparity suggests that the car's design must have been hopelessly muddled to cover the wide contingencies of mileage. A car designed to get high mileage cannot be the same car that is designed solely for performance. Design conflicts are guaranteed thereby. Sure enough, the smallest engine doesn't give the car much basic performance. But the biggest gives it too much. However, in the middle engines, for example, the 318-CID V-8 with 230 horsepower, the EPA says you get about 16.5 miles per gallon, with perfectly adequate performance.

Charger in 1974 now lists for $600 to $1,400. With the liability of poor sight lines, thanks to rear window design, bulbous rear end, and the reputation for guzzling gas because of the most common engine you will encounter—one of the big V-8s—this car should be bought for rock-bottom prices, if at all. Nevertheless, cars such as Challenger and Charger have a way of turning up on car buff lists. They could become interesting collector's items.

Charger/Magnum cars from 1975 to 1979 by Dodge, were "personal luxury" cars. They were the Dodge versions of Cordoba. Their prices range this way:

Year	Prices
1975	$1,000–$1,850
1976	$1,100–$2,000
1977	$1,800–$2,625
1978	$2,400–$3,400
1979	$3,100–$4,250

Dodge Coronet was a family car that started its modern life in 1971. That ended in 1974, like a lot of other things. Dodge Monaco took over for Coronet in 1975, lasting until 1978.

A wheelbase of 118 for the four-door sedan, 115 for the coupe, and the regular constellation of Chrysler Corporation engine choices made this car either a sluggish, pretty good customer on environmental scores with an EPA rating of 18 MPG using the slant-six engine, or a dullard with the big V-8 305 horsepower engine. That one got 12.1 MPG, according to the EPA.

A 1974 Coronet could cost $500 or $1,000, officially. It would be wise to use your best rust detector on mid-70s Chryslers, in order to get the lowest price.

The Monaco is similar in all respects, though it was changed cosmetically. Prices are as follows:

Year	Prices
1975	$ 575–$1,400
1976	$ 850–$1,700
1977	$1,325–$2,500
1978	$1,800–$3,100

Note that these cars are in the 4,000-pound weight class. The slant-six engine, though saving on gas, also saves on performance. It skimps. However, you do get a big, luxury car. If possible, find one of the smaller V-8 engines, say the 318-CID or the 360-CID. It might not be possible. People loved the bigger engines.

Two other Dodge cars, Diplomat and Mirada, were identical with Chrysler LeBaron and, in the case of Mirada, the 1980 Cordoba. All are departed. See those cars in the foregoing discussion under Chrysler. Everything is the same, including prices.

We have talked enough about Omni, but here are a few statistics: On a wheelbase of 99.2 inches, weight of 2,167 pounds, rear leg room of 33 inches, and EPA rating of 26.7 MPG, and ample room for four adults, the Omni/Horizon lists as follows:

Year	Prices
1978	$3,100–$4,000
1979	$3,750–$4,875
1980	$4,400–$5,600

These official prices vary enormously, and in some places you can't find a 1978 Omni for less than $4,000.

The Omni 024 is a racy version, mechanically identical,

FIGURE 36. Dodge Omni De Tomaso is a sporty hatchback version. It can hold golf bags in the rear, but people present another problem; and if that's your problem, the four-door version is preferable.

slightly more expensive. It started in 1979. It has virtually no back-seat capacity, unless you are a baby or a dwarf. Some dimensions outside differ also. The wheelbase is 96.7 inches. The external length in 173.3 inches, which is longer than the more spacious Omni, with an overall length of 164.8. But the racy exterior burns up those extra inches.

The Plymouth retinue begins with such cars as Barracuda, Fury, Gran Fury, Satellite, Valiant, and Volare. These cars all had twins elsewhere in the corporate lineup. The latest Plymouth is Horizon, an Omni clone, and Reliant, an Aries clone.

Barracuda died in 1974. It was a small car for those times, on a wheelbase of 108 inches, a length of 186.6 inches, and a weight of 3,255 pounds. It had no rear leg room to speak of (28.9 inches). Its repertory of engines ran from the slant six through almost every V-8 engine ever made by Chrysler. The most common engines were the six and the 318-CID V-8. With these engines the car was fairly economical, getting from 16.4 to 18 MPG, EPA numbers. The big bruiser engines were discontinued after 1971. Prices on the 1974 are listed as $750 to $1,400.

Plymouth Fury was a twin of Dodge Monaco and Polara. It expired in 1973. Replacing it were the Plymouth Fury and Gran Fury whose careers progressed from 1974 through 1977. They actually differed little from the earlier Plymouth Fury. One hesitates to use the term *evolution* with cars. It implies some kind of environmental adaptation, which cars are congenitally disqualified from attaining. The four-door sedan Fury is a huge bulk of a car, awkward, ungainly, rather stupid looking. Car designers in those days must have been mad fugitives from the Bauhaus School taking their revenge by creating severely ugly contours and details, devoid of ornamentation, grace, warmth, and especially utility. These designers showed how it is possible to avoid both ornamentation and utility.

The big Fury (Gran Fury) between 1974 and 1977 should be bought (if at all) for low dollars. Prices:

Year	Prices
1974	$ 400–$1,000
1975	$ 525–$1,400
1976	$ 900–$1,725
1977	$1,500–$2,400

Real world prices should be less. Be wary, especially, of large rust problems.

In 1980 a Gran Fury more or less identical with Chrysler Newport appeared, with that car's elegance of design. Its list prices are between $3,900 and $5,525.

Plymouth's Horizon, as noted, is identical with Omni, except for the grille. So are prices.

Plymouth TC3, a 1979 entrant, is identical with Omni 024, though one observer noted that it is much more attractive than the Omni 024 with its "gee-whiz" tape stripes and silly back window "louvers," but beauty is in the eye of the beholder.

Plymouth Horizon, if it can be bought at the right price, with the right low mileage, has to be considered one of the best cars in the world along with Omni. Most of the worst faults of

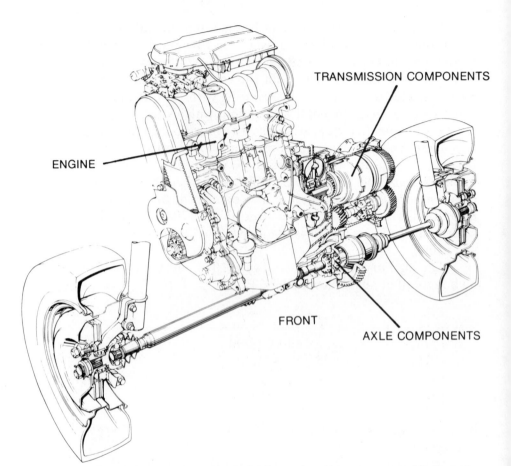

TRANSMISSION COMPONENTS

ENGINE

FRONT

AXLE COMPONENTS

FIGURE 37. Drawing of the Chrysler 2.2-liter engine which powers many of the front-drive cars in various lines. It shows how everything sits above the front axle, making for better traction.

the Rabbit engine were removed by 1978, and the only trick is to find one that rides, runs, and shifts smoothly and doesn't have a fuel pump that is about to destroy the engine. Chrysler is silent on the subject of whether or not that fuel pump has been redesigned. If it has not, I recommend that anyone buying such a car also buy a new fuel pump. Any mechanic will install one for $30, or you can buy one for $12 from the J. C. Whitney mail-order-parts catalog and install it yourself in twenty minutes. It is as easy as pie to do. Also, listen especially for engine vibration and roughness at various speeds. That is one additional problem that means early engine overhaul.

The fuel pump problem should be put in perspective. Probably the number of defective pumps in the several million cars out there is in the low thousands or less—a few hundred, perhaps. It isn't like rust damage, which will overtake every car on the road sooner or later. It isn't even like an exhaust system that inevitably self-destructs soon after 30,000 miles, or even before. Every part on a car can break or wear out, at almost any mileage. Most parts do not. We have identified the most likely breakdowns in the first part of the book. Beyond the more or less general system vulnerabilities we specify there, one must trust to luck. The human carcass has many parts that wear out or break down long before actuarial tables claim they should. Unusual stresses leading to these breakdowns may be identified in some cases—for example, smoking and lung cancer. But many cases cannot be so identified. Somewhat similar considerations apply to cars.

Plymouth Satellite is long departed (1974), with no significant number of mourners apparent. It ended in 1974 with a 117-inch wheelbase on the four-door sedan, 115 on the coupe. With curb weights of 3,350 and 3,320, and mostly V-8 engines, it did little to enhance gas supplies. It was not the worst offender in this matter when the slant-six engine was installed, which wasn't often.

Satellite prices for the last year are $500 to $1,100. Anything older than 1974 models would be interesting only to a restorer. Prices would be between $300 and $1,000.

Plymouth Valiant is identical with Dart, as are its prices. So is Plymouth Volare and Dodge Aspen.

To sum up one opinion about these cars; they were among the best cars produced in the world during the 1970s. Not notable for gas savings, they were also not notable guzzlers. As used cars they can be recommended with the usual warnings: rust on fenders, which can be repaired quite readily unless already done under the recall order; then the usual systematic examination of the breakdown systems.

Chrysler has turned itself around, and the big land yachts

of yore are now the small front-drive economy cars, with some luxuries of appointment. Yet Newport/New Yorker continue on in a much smaller guise. The newest versions of these grand old cars will deceive nobody into thinking they are the big V-8s of the 1970s, but they have some amenities and still carry the name.

FORD

Ford is the second name in U.S. automobiles, like Chicago in cities. Just as Chicago is basically contemptuous of its assigned role among cities, so Ford has been pleased to go its own sweet way in cars. This has been good and bad. Ford failed to understand the meaning of the turn to small front-drive cars, because it had always sold big rear-drive cars and nobody could tell Ford to change. It would be like telling Chicago to change. Whom would you tell? When the idea was broached to Henry Ford II, he politely turned it down.

Ford, like GM, decided to let others make those unprofitable small cars. Ford would skim the cream off the top, as it had in world markets. It would take more than an Arab sheik to shrink Ford cars. Ford turned out to be weak on history, long on stubbornness. This is not the happiest prescription for automotive success, as Ford is finding out to its regret. It remains to be seen what the ultimate fate of Ford will be. Unlike Chrysler, it has plenty of money. It has yet to overcome the lack of product.

Ford's belated appearance in the front-drive field centers on Escort and Mercury Lynx. The car is too new for much detailed performance data and systems analysis. It has had both good and bad reports. The automatic transmission is not recommended because of the inevitable sluggishness with the 1.6-liter engine. The stick shift works much better. Mileages are good, with 30 in the city, and up to 44 on the highway. So far, you can only buy it as a two-door hatchback or four-door wagon. The car is a 1981 debutant. Its prices range from

FIGURE 38. Ford's front-drive Escort and Mercury Lynx is a U.S. car with great gas mileage (up to 44 on highway, 30 city) and represents Ford's debut in front-drive cars.

$5,689 to $6,357. When it's a used car, you can expect to knock off at least $1,000.

Ford Escort/Lynx weighs 2,050 pounds, the four-cylinder 1.6-liter engine has a 98-CID 65-horsepower. The car, in driving tests, is a middle-range performer, neither one of the quickest nor one of the slowest. The high-gear ratio of 2.91 is about in the middle of small-engine cars, which means lower acceleration and better mileage in high gear. So it's middle brow, and driving confirms that the engine turns a few more times to get the same distance from standing start and takes a little extra gas. But these are not crucial, other than to note that if you drive a lot in the country, you will get better mileages than similar cars but not as good in the city, when it takes extra gas to get started, especially if you're in a hurry. Compare, for example, the numbers of a similarly powered car, the front-drive Omni. Omni gets slightly better than 22 MPG in city driving but about 38 in country. Omni also has more pep at traffic lights. However, the engines have similar power, and these are trivial differences and would depend on individual drivers.

Ford has had terrible publicity over one small car, Pinto,

which it may or may not have deserved. Ford didn't get good publicity over Fairmont, which it did deserve.

Fairmont was priced to compete with cars such as the Nova, Volare, Aspen, Concord, and so on. Many car buffs believe it to be the best of the entire lot. Considering that it was a forward-looking car in many ways, it exemplified Ford's refusal to go to front drive at a time when pressures were building for that configuration. Fairmont is a compact car in size, on a wheelbase of 105.5 inches, with overall length of 195.5 inches. It weighs close to 2,700 pounds, with good rear leg room of 35.3 inches. Using the recommended engine, a 200-CID six-cylinder, the mileage is about 20 MPG according to the EPA. The four-cylinder engine offers better mileage (23.6 MPG) and poorer performance. The car exemplifies state-of-the art rear drive, with innovative use of space and suspension details rivaling the front-drive technology that is supposed to be inherently better in these and other matters. Prices:

Year	Prices
1978	$2,600–$4,000
1979	$3,100–$4,750
1980	$3,900–$5,600
1981	$6,091–$6,735

Ford Granada, supposed to resemble Mercedes, didn't. This was fortunate in matters of price, less so in performance. A rather plushy compact car, it was on a wheelbase of 109.9 inches, with an overall length of 197.7 and a curb weight of about 3,200 pounds. Fuel economy with the 250 CID six-cylinder engine was good, rated by the EPA at close to 19 MPG. Inevitably the EPA and the average driver won't agree; mileages were widely reported well below official figures. It's an old story; the bureaucracy has one view, the real world another. However, Granada is not a small car by today's standards. For what it is, the car's mileage is good. Prices are as follows:

Year	Prices
1975	$1,200–$2,100
1976	$1,700–$2,650
1977	$2,200–$3,300
1978	$2,800–$4,000
1979	$3,300–$4,600
1980	$4,100–$5,450
1981	$6,474–$7,148

The newest Granada is now a different car, down-sized in 1981 to be identical with Fairmont, Mercury Cougar, and Zephyr. The wheelbase is now 106 inches; overall length is 196; and the weight, as with Fairmont, is around 2,700 pounds. Prices, as you can see from the foregoing, rose rather sharply in this transformation. Smaller is better.

Ford LTD and its Mercury Marquis twin are large cars by today's standards, but how the once mighty have fallen in girth. The older LTD and Marquis were big guzzlers, especially between 1973 and 1978. These cars are on 121-inch wheelbases, overall length of 219.6 inches, weight about 4,300 pounds. They are spacious and plush, with engines up to 460

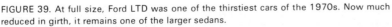
FIGURE 39. At full size, Ford LTD was one of the thirstiest cars of the 1970s. Now much reduced in girth, it remains one of the larger sedans.

CID, at 267 horsepower, with about 9 MPG if you drive mincingly. Smaller engines raised mileage all the way up to 15 MPG or better, so says the EPA, but like Detroit their guarantees aren't entirely reliable. The engine capable of this miracle is the 302 CID.

Prices of LTD (and Marquis) are:

Year	Prices
1974	$ 750–$1,375
1975	$ 900–$1,600
1976	$1,250–$2,100
1977	$1,800–$2,700
1978	$2,500–$3,525

LTD and Marquis went from a 121-inch wheelbase down to 114.3 in the 1979 transformation. Length is 209.3 inches. Weight is now about 3,600 pounds. Engines are three soft-spoken V-8s; 302, with 133 horses, rated at 15.4 MPG; a 351 CID rated at 142 horses with 13.9 MPG, and another 351 V-8 with 151 horses, with the same mileage rating. (The nine extra horses creep in via the carburetor.)

These cars are priced thusly:

Year	Prices
1979	$3,200–$5,300
1980	$3,900–$6,200
1981	$7,743–$8,775

As modern cars go, these biggies are good values. So long as you don't expect gas savings, you will get an enormous amount of creature comfort and automotive elan, for comparatively low prices. They are examples of Detroit doing what it can do best. A world under OPEC guns won't see it as a superlative automotive act, but it is.

Ford's Maverick, which ran its course from 1971 to 1977 and preceded the Fairmont, was a compact car with good mileage for the period. It butted heads with Dodge Dart and

Plymouth Valiant, Chevrolet Nova, and so on. These were all good, rather boring cars, but they got middle America through the muddled 1970s. Maverick was on a wheelbase of 103 inches for the two-door sedan, 109.9 inches for the four-door. Overall lengths had a similar bifurcation: 187 and 193.9 inches for two- and four-door cars. Weights were about 3,000 and 3,100. In the two-door sedan there was inadequate rear seat leg room (31.8), whereas in the four-door sedan leg room was 36 inches, which is quite enough.

Engines in Maverick were three Ford six-cylinder engines, and the 302 V-8. The sixes were the 170, 200, and 250 CID engines, with horsepower of 105, 75–97, and 85–98. The V-8 was the 302 CID with 122 to 143 horsepower. The EPA rated these engines at 19 MPG for the 170 CID; 17 to 20 for the 200; 16 to 19.5 for the 250, and 14 to 17 MPG for the V-8. It is idle to second-guess the EPA, but your chances of duplicating these mileages are slender.

Ford Maverick was a car that held its head high in the compact car sweepstakes of the 1970s. It had great acceptance, based in part on the various spinoff special cars, such as "Grabber" and "Stallion," which were Mavericks with a dose of terminal ostentation. However, Maverick had a broad and deep acceptance on its own. For a used car you can do a lot worse. Prices:

Year	Prices
1974	$ 850–$1,400
1975	$1,200–$1,875
1976	$1,600–$2,600
1977	$1,950–$2,800

Ford Mustang was a 1960s car dragged sneering into the 1970s. Mustang was a "muscle" car, a technical term impossible to define in 1980s parlance. It rivaled such cars as Camaro. These cars featured comparatively small bodies with huge, overpowered engines. They were not sports cars, as we know them today. They had no space, so they certainly weren't conveyances. You couldn't put a family in them, excepting a

FIGURE 40. Ford Mustang has evolved into this sporty sports coupe from its early muscle car image.

family of pigeons. Nobody knows why they were bought or who bought them, but apparently everybody did. Mustang was probably the most successful single car of the 1960s. Fortunately, this odd perversity vanished before our rational times had to cope with it. Few of these Mustangs exist today. But in case you want to do some historical slumming, you couldn't go more wrong than in a 1960s Mustang, a car to which history owes a debt of ingratitude. Ford had just discovered young women, to whom it addressed the Mustang in its advertising copy. Whether it was trying to do away with them or convert them was never clear.

Mustang II flourished between 1974 and 1978. It was much reduced from the proportions of Mustang I. The new car had a four-cylinder, overhead cam engine, a far cry from the muscle V-8s of its purple past. The engine next up the line was a six-cylinder Capri model. Made in Germany, this engine had an unusual series of problems for a German engine of the times; it was terrible. A 302-CID V-8 engine hardly cured matters, and it burned a lot of gas, that being the nature of the V-8.

Mustang II statistics: wheelbase 92.6 inches, length 175, weight 2,750 pounds. The official prices, as I stress repeatedly, are ballpark numbers.

158

Year	Prices
1974	$1,000–$2,000
1975	$1,400–$2,500
1976	$1,650–$3,000
1977	$2,100–$3,975
1978	$3,000–$4,400

Mustang changed again in 1979 for the better. It was based on Fairmont and became more or less identical with Capri (Mercury). With a four-cylinder engine of 140 CID, rated at 88 horsepower, and with a curb weight of about 2,600 pounds, the Mustang-Capri has a new career.

The wheelbase is 100.4 inches, overall length is 179.1 inches and weight is 2,530 pounds. Remember that these cars have no room for passengers in the rear seat—just room only for bags of groceries.

Mustang is supposed to fight Celica and GM and Chrysler sporty cars. The car is too new to determine whether or not it can go the distance in this fight. With the small engines it gets excellent mileages well over 22 MPG (EPA). If you buy one of the several V-8 engines, you won't come close to that number. Prices are:

Year	Prices
1979	$3,500–$5,300
1980	$4,400–$6,000
1981	$6,230–$6,789

Ford Pinto ended its career in a blaze, not of glory but of immolation. The lawsuit that spread the infamy of Pinto across the land, for killing its three teen-aged occupants, concealed all the important facts. Its gas tank, which exploded, was placed exactly like most other tanks of the times, out near the rear bumper which bashed it.

However, Pinto was ripe for retirement. It spanned the 1970s, obstinately persisting in the face of the blasting winds of change. Other than survival, it had few endearing qualities. It was a small car, not roomy and with the fuel-efficient engine (the overhead cam four-cylinder adopted in 1974 after complaints of sluggishness), the mileages were not bad, not great. It had an EPA rating of 23.2 to 24.3, which begins with the catalytic converter use in 1974–75. That was with the new four-cylinder engine. When you bought the newer V-6 engine, beginning in 1975, the mileages dropped to 18.6, again EPA. Whether anyone other than the EPA could get such mileage is doubtful.

Pinto's wheelbase is 94.5 (the wagon 94.8), its length is 170.8 (wagon 180.6), it weighs 2,070 (wagon 2,550). Rear-seat leg room is 29.5-inches—inadequate. Prices:

Year	Prices
1974	$ 700–$1,425
1975	$1,200–$1,900
1976	$1,400–$2,800
1977	$2,000–$3,400
1978	$2,500–$4,000
1979	$3,000–$4,450
1980	$3,400–$4,900

Thunderbird is a name that persists for a car that doesn't. It started as a Corvette rival, conceded defeat quickly, then withdrew to lick its wounds. The car of the 1972–76 run was the same as the Continental Mark IV in most ways. It had a wheelbase of 120.4 inches, a length of 216, and a weight of 4,585 pounds. These are classic guzzler dimensions, and if the bib fits, wear it, so the slogan might go. Plenty of people did and do. There is no lack of reasons, including those we have stated earlier at some length. For an occasional car you can hardly do better. Oscar Wilde's "only a fool fails to judge by appearances" applies to cars, and the appearance of these cars

FIGURE 41. Thunderbird is a name that will not die even though the original sports car did, decades ago. It is a personal luxury car to the manner born.

drew raves pro and con. Their ornamentation was not exactly Baroque, but it was not restrained either. It certainly wasn't refined. In the old days cars had tail fins, and while it was hard to justify them because the evolutionary history of mankind from the fish or seagoing state did not also include cars, it was even harder to justify Thunderbird's opera windows. Opera windows are for concealment, display, and for *La Traviata*. They are not for cars because they interfere with visibility, severely. Thunderbird has opera windows. If you like opera, you will hate opera windows—they have nothing to do with it—but the converse does not apply. So who likes opera windows? Designers, that's who.

Gas mileages of the mid-1970s Thunderbird were about 9 MPG.

The 1977–79 Thunderbird resembled LTD II. On a wheelbase of 114, with a length of 215.5 inches and a weight of 4,263, it was the big intermediate car. Its engines were all V-8s, from 302 to 400 CID. Mileages picked up, going as high as EPA's estimated 15.1 with the 302 engine. That would be coasting slowly on a smooth road. Prices:

Year	Prices
1977	$2,300–$3,200
1978	$2,800–$4,100
1979	$3,600–$4,900

Lightning struck again, in 1980, decreasing Thunderbird by a thousand pounds, down to 3,200, shaving it off to a wheelbase of 108.4 and a length of 200.4. Two engines are its lot; a 255-CID V-8 and the bigger 302. Mileages are now rated at 17 and 18.2 MPG. Prices:

Year	Prices
1980	$4,500–$6,000
1981	$6,535–$6,694

Note that Mercury Cougar is now a twin of Thunderbird, as are its vital statistics. Because it is also related to the basic Fairmont structure and mechanical systems, it has become a fairly modern car. It is, of course, rear drive.

Ford Torino was an intermediate car of the mid 1970s that continues to populate the lots. It was not a distinctive car; it had descended from the earlier Fairlane, which also wasn't distinctive. On a wheelbase of 114 inches (two-door) and 118 inches (four-door), the curb weights were 3,450 and about 3,800 for the two different body styles. Engines were the entire repertory of V-8s, from the 302-CID to the 460, the latter an engine with an insatiable lust for gas and go. About the only thing that set Torino apart was the slightly greater heft it had over other intermediates of the time. In the annals of distinctions that one doesn't cut much ice, as of this day. Prices for Torino:

Year	Prices
1975	$650–$1,450
1976	$975–$1,825

Lincoln/Mercury cars were a full line through the 1970s, until the later stretches, when OPEC cut them down to size. Lincoln Continental was the flagship. In 1975 it underwent a slight weight reduction but remained an almost 5,000-pound car on a 127.2-inch wheelbase. These statistics survived through 1979. Just as there is nothing like a dame, so there is nothing like a big Continental. It is self-limiting, in a way. With Cadillac you had some limitations of luxury forced on it by competition from the other big GM cars. Continental was free to pursue the lap of luxury, which it did with yachtlike dedication. Overall length was 225 inches, which is almost 7-feet longer than Le Car. A car almost 19 feet long, weighing more than twice the typical subcompact—now the norm for mass transportation— clearly was not destined for immortality, though it continues to find favor in some Arab countries, where gas presents a somewhat different problem than it does here.

Lincoln had only one engine in the period under review, the 460 CID. Nothing less would move it. Prices list as follows:

Year	Prices
1975	$1,475–$2,400
1976	$2,300–$3,475
1977	$3,500–$4,800
1978	$4,700–$6,200
1979	$6,200–$8,000

These prices are meaningless. If you bought a 1975 Continental in poor condition, you could spend $3,000 to get it into a condition befitting such a car. Anyone contemplating the purchase of such a car should bear in mind the costs of renovation, and every six- or seven-year-old car needs renovation.

Lincoln Continental of 1980 is on a wheelbase of 117.3 inches, an overall length of 219 inches, with a weight of about 4,000 pounds. Engines are the 302 and 351 V-8s. Mileages have doubled over the earlier guzzler, to about 12.2 MPG. However, once a guzzler always a guzzler, in the Lincoln Continental scheme of things. Prices:

Year	Prices
1980	$ 8,200–$10,100
1981	$17,237–$23,217

These prices do not connote your average people's car market. They also show that earlier Continentals retain high dollar values, if renovation isn't excessive.

The Lincoln Versailles made its debut in 1977. It is a luxury version of the Ford Granada and Mercury Monarch, with V-8 engine; both 302 and 351-CID will be found. Prices:

Year	Prices
1977	$4,000–$ 5,500
1978	$5,100–$ 6,600
1979	$6,600–$ 8,275
1980	$8,450–$10,500

Obviously the car is overpriced because Granada and Monarch cost a lot less and aren't a lot less car. The differences are in luxuries and cosmetics. The car was supposed to compete with Seville by Cadillac. It didn't. It's gone.

The Lincoln Mark series of cars were floating harem designs; the Everleigh Sisters of early Chicago ill fame must have had these cars in mind when they designed their opulent houses of pleasure. These cars have so many electrical appliances in them and so many power-driven devices that it almost requires the services of a full-time electrician to keep them going. Bear that in mind when you shop in their bailiwick.

Mark III dates from 1971, which is prehistory. But Mark IV will be found from 1975 and 1976. These cars are a lot like Thunderbird of the times. So are the prices and statistics.

Mark V, from 1977 to 1979, is on a wheelbase of 120.4 inches, as the earlier car was. It is lighter by about 200 pounds, but the length is about 2 inches longer. The car is essentially the same as the earlier one, with one smaller engine. The standard engine is the 400 CID, with the 460 optional. Prices are:

Year	Prices
1977	$4,200–$5,800
1978	$5,500–$7,250
1979	$7,100–$9,000

Mark VI is the same car as the 1980 Lincoln. At this point all the bigger Ford Corporation products—LTD and Marquis— are much alike. That includes Lincoln and Mark VI. Wheelbase is 114.3 inches for the two-door coupe and 117.3 inches for the newly minted four-door sedan—a puzzling family addition to the harem ambience of the Mark image and decor.

Mark VI 1980 ranges in price from $9,500 to $11,500. In 1981 prices are $17,237 to $23,217, like Continental. The only difference between these cars is that the two-door model is on a shorter wheelbase, as noted previously, compared with the four-door.

Mercury Lynx is identical with Ford Escort; Cougar and Granada are twins, Marquis and LTD are twins, so are Capri and Mustang. Specifications and prices are either identical or so close as to be indistinguishable.

GENERAL MOTORS

General Motors has dominated world automotive production, design, sales, and marketing for so long that it is a shock to realize how this company, not many years ago the biggest in the U.S., has fallen on bad times. Without pretending that any summary can explain the red ink position GM is in versus the Japanese, one may say that General Motors is in no danger of imminent decline in market share. Unfortunately, it has lost its once dominant role overseas, but even there it continues to play an important role. Perhaps that role will expand, given the expanding repertory of new, front-drive cars introduced by GM in recent years, with the promise of more to come. GM is the only U.S. car company in a position to compete worldwide with the Japanese, and the only limitations on its role will come from financial or governmental considerations.

Buick, Cadillac, Chevrolet, Pontiac, and Oldsmobile can be discussed separately, but the fact is that they not only overlap, but they also duplicate models.

Buick Apollo, Buick Skylark, and Chevrolet Nova are triplets. Millions of these cars in their larger, heavier versions dating from 1968 to 1974 are on the streets chugging away. Later, they were "down-sized." Though we have been saying that anything earlier than 1975 isn't worth talking about, it is hard to ignore the tons of these cars in service.

FIGURE 42. The Nova, in its 1979 "down-sized" version, is more economical and not as roomy as the earlier, heavier car.

On a wheelbase of 111 inches, overall length of 200.3 inches, and weight of about 3,350 pounds, these cars are large by today's standards but compact or smallish by early 1970s thinking.

The 1974 lists for $1,000 to $1,700, but few of them would sell for such prices. They would have heavy mileage, worn out main systems, much body rust, and little real value, unless you could find that "garage-kept" car that shows up in the ads more than in life. Even so, beware a '74 car with low mileage. If it has been out of service for years, the shock of sudden activation would almost certainly cause major breakdowns of engine and transmission. How else could a '74 car have low mileage? Engines were the six-cylinder 250 or the 350 V-8, the most famous engine in the world. There were two of them on this car, the V-8 with two-barrel carburetor rated at 150 horsepower and the four-barrel V-8 with 175 horses.

The 1975–79 Skylark has basic dimensions and statistics identical with earlier models, but there are a few differences. Suspension has been changed and the V-6 engine made standard thus increasing gas mileage. The repertory of engines is broadened and includes a long line of V-8s, including the inevitable 350s. The car is identical with Chevrolet Nova, once again. Prices:

Year	Prices
1975	$1,300–$2,300
1976	$1,800–$3,000
1977	$2,400–$3,600
1978	$2,700–$4,100
1979	$3,300–$4,600

The Skylark became the X-body front-drive car in 1980. Buick Apollo disappeared somewhere along the line; actually it was merged with Skylark in 1975.

FIGURE 43. Malibu is one of a large GM family that includes cars such as the Cutlass, Century, and Special.

Buick Century, Regal, and Special, are a trio of cars very much alike; also, Oldsmobile Cutlass, Chevrolet Chevelle, and Malibu. These cars have more in common than not. They share engines, transmissions, and many other components. They may not all look alike, and there are enough differences of suspension tuning and details to keep their "feel" slightly different, but they all come from the same basic design and components. One may have one engine choice, the other may have a slightly different one. GM has to have options to set one line of cars off from another. Thus, for example, the '75 Buick Century Special has the V-6 engine by itself that year.

Wheelbases on these cars are 112 inches for the two-door, 116 inches for the four-door sedan. Overall length is 210.7 inches and 212.4 inches. Wagons are somewhat different, especially in weight, inevitably. Weights are close to 4,000 pounds, 400 more in the station wagons. Engines begin with the 231 V-6, but most of these cars had one of the 350 V-8 engines, with two- or four-barrel carburetors. The big 455-CID engines were options. Prices:

Year	Prices
1975	$1,200–$2,125
1976	$1,700–$2,600
1977	$2,200–$3,500

The 1978 change in Century produced a car with a wheelbase of 108.1 inches, a length of 196, and weight of 3,200 pounds (100 more for the 4-door sedan and wagon). This car, with the V-6 engine, gets about 20 MPG. Prices:

Year	Prices
1978	$2,700–$4,000
1979	$3,300–$4,850
1980	$4,500–$5,800
1981	$7,619–$8,226

These prices refer also to Chevrolet Malibu, Oldsmobile

Cutlass, and Pontiac LeMans. Differences among them are mostly cosmetic.

These cars represent General Motors in transition to the front-drive versions, yet they remain standards in the world for cars of the size, drivability, ridability, and systems design. As used cars, they can be among the best values. Parts are comparatively inexpensive—GM parts always are—from a third to half the cost of import parts, for example. Mechanics always know how to fix them, and generally they aren't difficult to repair.

Buick Electra and Oldsmobile 98 commenced life in 1971, felt the sting of OPEC in 1977, and held on to much of the early heft. Though the car lost 1,000 pounds and 9 inches of wheelbase, it is not exactly anemic today.

The mid-'70s Electra and Olds 98 had a wheelbase of 127 inches, an overall length of 226.2 inches, and a weight of between 4,725 pounds at the least to almost 4,900 for the biggest. Engines were two V-8s, the 350 with four-barrel carburetor; the 455, also with four-barrel. Gas mileages with the 350 engine were 15 MPG (EPA), dropping to 11–13 with the bigger engine. Olds 98 engines were the 400 and 455 V-8s. Prices also apply to Olds 98:

Year	Prices
1975	$1,100–$1,900
1976	$1,700–$2,600

The 1977 Electra and Oldsmobile 98 are on a wheelbase of 118.9 inches, with overall length of 222.1 inches, weight of about 3,950 to 4,225 pounds for the station wagon. Engines begin with the 252-CID V-6, ascending through three V-8s, including the 301-, 350-, and 403-CID engines. One of the 350s has fuel injection, with a horsepower rating of 105, beginning in the 1980 model year. That earned it an EPA rating of 25 MPG. (The same applies to Olds 98, but with 23 MPG rating.) Don't hold your breath waiting for that mileage. Prices:

Year	Prices
1977	$ 2,700–$4,000
1978	$ 3,700–$5,200
1979	$ 4,700–$6,700
1980	$ 6,400–$8,800
1981	$10,538–$11,783

These prices also apply to the similar Oldsmobile 98.

Buick LeSabre, Centurion, and Olds Delta 88 are cars so similar to the cars just mentioned, yet below them in price, size, and so on that one wonders how they ever managed to squeeze into the GM marketing picture.

LeSabre/Centurion, between 1971 and 1976, were 124-inch wheelbase cars, 226.9 inches in length, weighing between 4,300 and 5,200 pounds (two-door up to big station wagon).

Engines were 231 V-6, 350 and 455 V-8s. Each V-8 could be bought with either two or four-barrel carburetors. Mileages were between 12 and 16.5 MPG. One is tempted to snort at these EPA figures, and one should. They are not real-world numbers, and it must be kept in mind when looking at these cars. Also, cars lose gas mileage as they age. A careful driver could get good mileages in some circumstances—for example, cruising at steady speeds on the highway, especially around 55 MPH. But who does that? These prices also apply to Centurion and Olds Delta 88.

Year	Prices
1975	$1,000–$2,100
1976	$1,500–$2,525

LeSabre was lightened and shortened ("down-sized") in 1977. Wheelbase is 116 inches, length is 217.4, weight is 3,475 to 3,575 pounds. Engines are the V-6, one with turbocharging in 1979–80. The long repertory of V-8 engines included one 350 with fuel injection that earned it an EPA mileage tag of 25

MPG. Generally, mileages were rated between 13 and 20 MPG. Prices:

Year	Prices
1977	$2,200–$3,600
1978	$2,700–$4,775
1979	$3,600–$5,500
1980	$4,500–$6,150
1981	$7,873–$8,906

Buick Regal, a "personal luxury" coupe beginning in 1978, is a Century-like posh car with a wheelbase of 108.1 inches, length of 200, weight of 3,200 pounds, with three V-6 engines and two V-8s. Turbocharging was featured on one of the V-6s with four-barrel carburetion. However, the best mileage was on the 196- and 231-CID V-6s, which were rated at up to 22 MPG. The V-8 engines were discontinued in 1980, and the biggest V-8 is found only in 1978. Regal, Chevrolet Monte Carlo, Olds Cutlass Supreme, and Pontiac Grand Prix are very similar cars. Prices:

FIGURE 44. Chevy Monte Carlo is related to Buick Regal, Pontiac Grand Prix, and the Olds Cutlass Supreme.

Year	Prices
1978	$3,500–$5,000
1979	$4,200–$5,600
1980	$5,000–$6,500
1981	$7,778–$8,834

These prices also apply to the other lines, but some differences in price will be found in the most recent cars, apart from differences based on condition, mileage, and optional equipment.

Buick Riviera, between 1971 and 1976, was a guzzler on a 122-inch wheelbase, 223 inches in length, 4,700 pounds in weight, with the 455-CID engine. Mileages are listed at 12 to 13.5. Prices:

Year	Prices
1975	$1,200–$2,000
1976	$1,800–$2,700

Riviera became a smaller car in 1977, and again in 1979. In 1977 it is similar to LeSabre in size. On a wheelbase of 115.9 inches, length of 218.2 inches, weight of about 4,000 pounds, it had engines of 350 and 403 CID and was rated at 16 and 14 MPG. Prices:

Year	Prices
1977	$3,000–$4,200
1978	$4,300–$5,600

Riviera became a front-drive car in 1979, sharing power train and other systems with Olds Toronado and Cadillac Eldorado. On a wheelbase of 114 inches, length of 206.6 inches, and weight of 3,875, the engines are the V-6 with turbocharging and the 350 V-8. Mileages are 18 and 17 MPG. Prices:

Year	Prices
1979	$ 6,600–$ 8,100
1980	$ 8,000–$10,400
1981	$12,523–$13,499

Buick Skyhawk, from 1975 to 1980, was a Monza-derived, sporty car, with Buick's V-6 engine as the only power plant available. Mileages were between 17 and 19. On a wheelbase of 97 inches, a length of 179.3, and curb weight of about 2,800 pounds, the car was not exactly competition for the imports, as it was designed to be, but it was a classy little car, nonetheless. Prices:

Year	Prices
1975	$1,400–$2,100
1976	$2,000–$2,900
1977	$2,400–$3,300
1978	$2,900–$3,900
1979	$3,600–$4,600
1980	$4,200–$5,350

FIGURE 45. The Monza and its Buick clone, the Skyhawk, had a common parent, the Vega. However, engines and other components were changed in order to hide the family resemblance.

Buick Skylark had a first career as an intermediate, with its brothers and sisters in all the other GM lines (Pontiac LeMans, Chevelle, Malibu, Cutlass, and so forth). Today, it is one of the front-drive X-body cars. First, the old one.

Skylark divided its 1970s career between intermediate status and compact. The compact size dates from 1975. That's the one of interest, though there are plenty of intermediates around, still going strong. Those early cars, with 350 V-8 engines, mostly, were great, durable performers, though they often had the two-speed automatic transmission, which was neither great nor durable. They go far back into the 1960s.

The 1975 Skylark was on a wheelbase of 111 inches, with overall length of 200.3 inches, with curb weight of about 3,450 pounds. Engines were almost everything in the GM line up to the 350 V-8. Best mileages were with the V-6 231 CID. That one is rated 19 MPG and remained the basic engine throughout Skylark's compact career. Prices:

Year	Prices
1975	$1,300–$2,300
1976	$1,800–$3,000
1977	$2,400–$3,600
1978	$2,700–$4,100
1979	$3,300–$4,600

It is impossible to find a better used car than Skylark. With the V-6 engine the car is Detroit at its best. No matter what system you examine on this car, you must be impressed. Even the body had very moderate rust tendencies. To be sure, 1975 was the first year of high-energy ignition, which replaced one of the best mechanical distributors ever devised. High-energy ignition has years to go before making us forget what it replaced.

Chevrolet Nova, Oldsmobile Omega, and Pontiac Ventura are either identical with or similar to Skylark.

Skylark 1980 is the revolutionary front-drive General Motors X-body car (also Chevrolet Citation, Oldsmobile Omega, and Pontiac Phoenix). Detroit will never be the same, after this car (and the other X's).

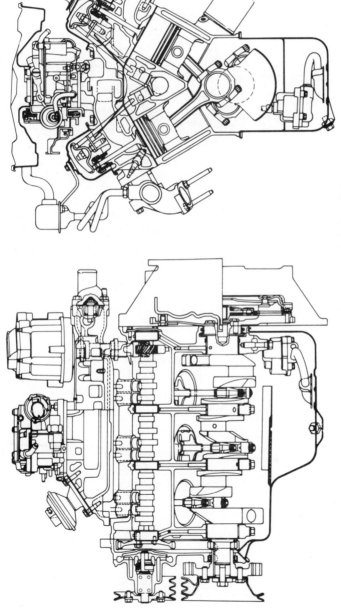

1980 CHEVROLET CITATION 60° V-6 ENGINE
TRANSVERSE SECTION

1980 CHEVROLET CITATION 60° V-6 ENGINE
LONGITUDINAL SECTION

FIGURE 46. Two views of the GM V-6 engine, the workhorse of most GM lines, including all the front-drive cars that don't use the four-cylinder, "iron duke" engine and its derivatives.

FIGURE 47. Chevrolet Citation regained GM's clout as an innovative competitor. Probably it is best to avoid the first ones, but recent X-body cars are among the world's best.

On a wheelbase of 104.9 inches, with overall length of 181.1 inches, and weight of about 2,500 pounds, the car uses space admirably enough to warrant it being designated a compact. The base engine is the overhead cam 151-CID four-cylinder, rated at 23 MPG. The V-6 is rated at 20 MPG and is optional. Prices:

Year	Prices
1980	$4,700–$6,300
1981	$6,405–$7,040

Note that Citation prices are less:

Year	Prices
1980	$4,300–$5,925
1981	$6,270–$6,404

Pontiac Phoenix:

Year	Prices
1980	$4,700–$6,300
1981	$6,307–$6,969

Olds Omega:

Year	Prices
1980	$4,700–$6,300
1981	$6,343–$6,855

Though the cars are identical, cosmetic features cause the minor differences in price.

Cadillac's Fleetwood has a wheelbase of 130 inches. Cadillac Cimarron's wheelbase is 101.2. Cimarron's overall length is 173 inches compared with Fleetwood's 230.7. Newer Fleetwood statistics slash about 9 inches away, to bring the length down to 221, but the almost 5 feet difference between the old Fleetwood and the new Cimarron tell visually and graphically how Cadillac has coped with OPEC. Barely.

Fleetwood, Calais, and DeVille, were basically the same car until 1976. That car, in addition to the numbers cited above, weighed about 5,400 pounds. It has 472- and 500-CID V-8 engines, rated at about 12 MPG. In real life you would expect about half that mileage. Prices:

Year	Prices
1975	$1,400–$2,400
1976	$2,300–$3,600

DeVille and Fleetwood went down to a wheelbase of 121.4 inches in 1977, with overall length of 221 inches and weight of about 4,500 pounds. Calais dropped out. More important, mileages were improved through the use of fuel injection with a 350 V-8 engine to the 21–23-MPG area—according to EPA. Three more powerful engines will be found in these cars. Prices:

Year	Prices
1977	$3,800–$5,400
1978	$5,200–$6,900
1979	$6,600–$9,200

Cadillac Eldorado, between 1975 and 1978, had a wheelbase of 126.3 inches, length of 224.1 inches, weight of 5,300, and engines of 425 and 500 CID. Mileages rated at 14 and 12–13. Prices:

Year	Prices
1975	$1,600–$2,700
1976	$2,300–$5,000
1977	$4,000–$5,800
1978	$5,200–$6,700

Eldorado was reduced further in 1979. It also became a front-drive car, with Olds Toronado and Riviera. Prices are:

Year	Prices
1979	$ 8,700–$11,200
1980	$10,500–$12,950
1981	$16,871

Compare Riviera prices, just mentioned. They are less. Engines offered include the V-8 engine that switches between four, six, and eight cylinders; the 350 V-8; and you can get the Oldsmobile diesel. Note that GM plans to junk the variable V-8 engine. It has been a pain in the neck.

Cadillac Seville commenced life as a Mercedes fighter, but the knowledge that it came out of the Chevy Nova stable didn't sustain it. The car it competes with between 1975 and 1979 is the Lincoln Versailles, also a car based on a much less expensive chassis.

Seville was on a wheelbase of 114.3 inches, with a length of 204 and weight of 4,300 pounds. Prices:

Year	Prices
1975	$4,000–$ 5,700
1976	$4,800–$ 6,300
1977	$5,800–$ 7,600
1978	$7,000–$ 8,850
1979	$8,500–$11,000

Seville, in 1980, became a front-drive car similar to or identical with Eldorado/Riviera/Toronado. In 1980 its prices are $12,000 to $14,500; in 1981 the price is $22,084, though it should be noted that the car will sell for both more and less. The dealer cost is $19,320.

Chevrolet, like apple pie and motherhood, has taken its licks. Corvair and Vega blackened its eye in the view of consumerists, who thought these cars were at best a ripoff and at worst (Corvair) murderous. Corvair is no longer an issue, having departed this vale of tears in 1969. Vega is very much an issue, with millions of them around. We have discussed it elsewhere. Its last year was 1977. On a wheelbase of 97 inches, with overall length of 169.7 inches, and weight of about 2,225 pounds, Vega was a real import fighter, unless you added the air conditioning, thus reducing gas mileages sharply down to levels that made the imports win. Nobody noticed that air conditioning had the same effect on gas mileages of imports. Admittedly, the last couple of years were Vega's best, but the 1975 wasn't all that terrible. Rust damage did indeed occur, as it does to all cars. Maybe Vega was worse than usual; maybe not. If you count panels, you might tote up a larger number of rust spots on a Vega than you would on (say) a Buick or Chrysler. But rust is where you find it; you find it everywhere on cars over three years of age. Until the cars are made of plastic or of intolerably expensive alloys, you will find rust. Fortunately you can fix it. Prices:

Year	Prices
1975	$ 800–$1,500
1976	$1,200–$2,000
1977	$1,600–$2,400

Camaro was Chevrolet's '70s car for making time with youth. It was spirited, too powerful, too small for passengers, too sporty, too low for convenient entering and exiting, which made it irresistible to certain age groups.

Camaro, Vega, and other small Chevrolets developed the kind of cult following that GM executives dreamt about. It had a wheelbase of 108 inches, length of 197.6, weight of 3,400 pounds, and 28.6-inch leg room in the rear seat. Virtually the whole repertory of GM engines powered it, beginning with the V-8s and going up to a 350 V-8 rated up to 275 horsepower, with four-barrel carburetor. Prices:

Year	Prices
1975	$1,600–$2,500
1976	$2,200–$3,125
1977	$2,500–$3,800
1978	$3,300–$4,800
1979	$4,000–$5,700
1980	$4,800–$7,100
1981	$6,780–$8,298

It should be noted, parenthetically, that Camaro and Firebird (another cult car) are hard to tell apart without a magnifying glass, but aficionados would consider such a remark blasphemy, idiocy, and worse.

Chevrolet Cavalier is a J-body car. That's the most recent front-drive after the X-body cars, but both will soon be supplanted by the A-body cars, including the Chevrolet Celebrity. Ciera is the Oldsmobile name, whereas Pontiac has run out of names and will call their car simply A6000, as if it is a prisoner.

Cavalier is a bit smaller than Citation but uses that car's transaxle, engine, and other components. However, it has the usual GM differentiation methods—its own suspension feel, though it's still the same suspension with MacPherson struts, and other touches. The wheelbase is 101.2, overall length 172.4, weight 2,460. These are all near or identical Citation numbers. The price, however, is exhibit A in the search for the cause and cure of a new national syndrome, "sticker shock." Prices are $6,966 to $8,452 for the five-door wagon. These prices are with standard equipment. When you start adding air conditioning at $625, automatic transmission for $370, AM/FM stereo radio for $100, power steering (essential) for $180, and various other goodies, it is easy to develop sticker shock in a hurry.

The newest Chevrolet, Celebrity, is also a systems clone

of Citation et al. It uses the same engine, transaxle, strut suspension, rack-and-pinion steering, and so on, but it will cost more, it will ride differently (more softly, no doubt), and won't be a used car for a while—so it will not detain us further.

All these Citation clones should be compared with prices on used Citations as they become used cars. No matter what promotion makes them out to be, at bottom they are Citations.

FIGURE 48. Caprice is a Cadillac in Chevrolet clothing. Along with Impala, it is the middle-class Cadillac.

Chevrolet Caprice and Impala have taken their lumps from earlier vintages when they had big wheelbase and other dimensions. In 1975 and '76 these were big cars. They weighed from 4,300 to almost 5,000 pounds, with 121.5-inch wheelbases, and lengths of 222.7 inches. Their engines were usually big, including most of the V-8s in the GM arsenal. Their mileages were not big. As used cars their prices are not big:

Year	Prices
1975	$ 900–$2,100
1976	$1,300–$2,550

Caprice and Impala came down to 116-inch wheelbases in 1977, along with LeSabre and other GM cars of the period.

Their weights dieted down also, to 3,700 pounds and up to 4,200 for the station wagon. Prices:

Year	Prices
1977	$2,000–$3,400
1978	$2,600–$4,300
1979	$3,300–$5,100
1980	$4,300–$6,200
1981	$7,210–$8,194

Caprice and Impala, after their 1977 revolution, or palace coup, did well enough with gas mileages to warrant their removal from the blacklist of cars unfit for the new era. With the V-6 they were rated at 20 MPG, and with fuel injection, 25.5 (EPA).

Many people regarded these cars as the best in the world. They were super-silky in performance; their new-found respect for gasoline, and their easy, coddling suspensions systems made them irresistible. A 1977 Caprice in the right condition is indeed a great buy—at the right price.

Chevelle, an intermediate, spent the middle 1970s (with Malibu) on a wheelbase of 112 (two-door coupe) and 116 inches (four-door) and a length of 202.9 and 206.9 (coupe versus sedan). Weights were 3,550 and 3,800 (same two cars) and 4,150 (wagon). Engines were the various V-8s mostly, and mileages were 12 to 15 or 16, with one engine, the in-line 6 getting 18. Prices:

Year	Prices
1975	$1,000–$2,000
1976	$1,500–$2,500
1977	$2,000–$3,150

Chevette, the biggest-selling car in the U.S., comes from GM's Opel hutch in Germany. The car is about as basic as you can get and continue to function well in the twentieth century. One suspects that in an earlier incarnation it was found under a

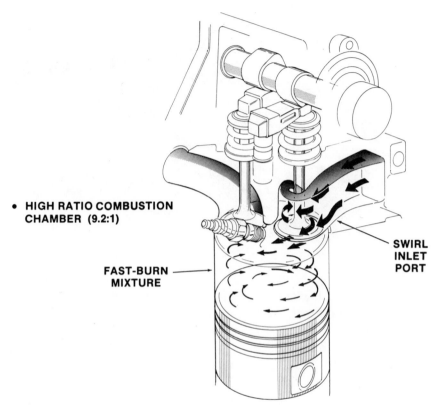

- **HIGH RATIO COMBUSTION CHAMBER (9.2:1)**

FAST-BURN MIXTURE

SWIRL INLET PORT

FIGURE 49. Chevette, one of the most popular cars in GM history, has a great four-cylinder engine with this configuration starting in the 1982 model.

rock near the earliest Toyota factory. It arrived in 1976 and continues to go great guns. It shows the power of an old idea: Keep it simple, stupid. Prices:

Year	Prices
1976	$1,600–$2,350
1977	$2,100–$2,800
1978	$2,700–$3,500
1979	$3,200–$4,200
1980	$3,800–$4,825
1981	$4,595–$5,294

FIGURE 50. If you've seen one Corvette, you haven't seen them all, but you get the general idea.

Corvette is lawless unto itself. Everything it does best is either illegal (too much speed) or immoral (too much gas); hence its popularity. Through most of the '70s Corvette was on a 98-inch wheelbase, 182.5 inches in length, 3,300 pounds of concentrated weight, and with a repertory of V-8 engines. The 350 V-8 in various carburetor pairings (all guzzling) did the deed, though you could also buy bigger engines up to the 425-horsepower V-8 between 1971 and 1974. May it rest in pieces.

A few minor changes occurred in 1978, but the car hasn't changed much in recent years. Prices:

Year	Prices
1975	$ 4,800–$ 6,000
1976	$ 5,400–$ 6,800
1977	$ 6,100–$ 7,700
1978	$ 7,400–$ 9,100
1979	$ 8,100–$10,000
1980	$ 9,500–$11,600
1981	$14,000

Malibu is a Chevrolet intermediate discussed earlier with Buick Century.

Monte Carlo also is discussed earlier with Buick Regal.

Monza, between 1975 and 1980, comes along with Vega as a fancier version. Through 1977 it had the Vega power train; then it received the Pontiac four-cylinder 151 CID, which is GM's basic four-cylinder engine with modifications wherever it appears.

The specifications follow Vega. Prices:

Year	Prices
1975	$1,300–$2,100
1976	$1,800–$2,600
1977	$2,200–$3,025
1978	$2,600–$3,800
1979	$3,000–$4,200
1980	$4,000–$5,100

This car has had a poor history; yet with the V-6 engine it has much to offer in economy, liveliness, and subcompact size.

Nova, as we observe elsewhere, was on a 111-inch wheelbase, weighing 3,300 pounds, and with fair gas mileages from the six-cylinder engines, less so with the V-8s, though the 260 CID was rated at 17 MPG. Its career ended in 1980. Prices:

Year	Prices
1975	$1,300–$2,300
1976	$1,800–$2,825
1977	$2,300–$3,400
1978	$2,900–$4,100
1979	$3,200–$4,400

Oldsmobile Cutlass has been an enormously successful car for reasons hard to understand. It was identical with Buick Skylark years ago, which it outsold consistently. Between 1973 and 1977, it joined Buick Regal and Century, to say nothing of the other GM intermediate lines. Now it is on the 108-inch wheelbase, which it shares with Camaro, Malibu, Monte Carlo, Regal, Century, Cutlass Supreme, Grand Prix, Firebird, and LeMans. It also joins such cars as Ford Thunderbird and

Mercury Cougar, AMC Concord and Eagle in this crowded number. It not only shares wheelbase numbers, it shares power trains, suspension systems (with the usual minor tuning differences), and other components up and down the GM line. There is no scandal about such sharing, despite the litigation over the Oldsmobile and Chevrolet engines that wound up in court to GM's disadvantage and that of the taxpayers. The courts, who ruled against GM, and the lawyers who brought the suits, caused the prices, taxes, wages and inflation to go up. And what goes down? Our ability to compete with Japan. So, we export our industry to Japan, with the jobs and our industrial base. Note that all Japanese automakers use the same kind of component sharing in their cars, but Japan has about 10 percent of the number of lawyers we are proud to claim. Indeed, if such sharing did not occur, the cars would cost twice as much or more—we would be even less competitive.

So, if it is hard to understand why Cutlass has been so successful, we must make the effort. One reason is that the interiors and exteriors caught the public fancy. People liked the cosmetics of the car. It also had a reputation for great highway authority and ridability, although its reputation was unsullied by any claim on behalf of gas mileage. Much of its reputation came from advertising that made people believe it had almost magical powers of durability. However, one thing was obvious to all: The car had better than average resale value simply because it was so highly prized.

Systems durability couldn't have been any better than other GM cars with which it shared components. The engines and transmissions, brakes, rear components, suspension, and steering systems were either identical with or similar to other GM intermediates. They were all durable, with the exceptions based on mileage and normal wear, as well as accidents, such as we noted earlier. If you examine the recall history, you can see that the car was not made in Plato's heaven as a perfect, ideal model for distantly related cars on earth. It turned up with a lot of recall citations. So, we come down to resale value and cosmetics. They are reasons enough, but the dominant years for Cutlass were also the last great years for GM before the OPEC assault took its final toll. Any GM car from the period was at least good for the money, and Oldsmobile was perceived to be better.

GM engines and transmissions are interchangeable and similar, but they do have slightly different interior designs and specifications on the cars they power. It is inevitable, given different capacities. A brief could be argued on behalf of engines that most often were associated with Cutlass. For example, they were certainly more durable than Vega, to take the opposite extreme.

The real competition was with Ford and Chrysler. Here the issue is clouded. Cutlass is no better than the competition at Ford and Chrysler. Its window gaskets and cement wear or jar loose, allowing rain to cause rust at all the familiar places. Its carburetors gradually gum up and wear out, causing all the usual fuel problems. Its water pump self-destructs and so on, but so do those at Ford and Chrysler. We deal with human-technological limits. It was no problem when gas was plentiful. Unfortunately today, when it is not, all the good qualities of these cars have faded.

Oldsmobile Cutlass mythology ultimately sold the car. Without examining it too closely, we must admit that image advertising created the basis of the mythology, slender as it was. The fact is, the car doesn't sell for more than others of similar systems and cosmetics. As to preferences based on luxuries and appointments, nobody can gainsay them: They are personal. As noted, the car had as many recalls as others, whatever weight attaches to that. So, we are left with the Cutlass image. Maybe it was the name. Name associations become irrational and motivating. But a cutlass? A pirate, perhaps? Who needs pirates? Perhaps we all need piracy or secretly hope to practice a little on the side.

Whatever, we are left with the legend and the car.

It was on the 112-inch wheelbase for the two-door coupe, and 116 for the four-door sedan and wagon. It was 207 and 211 inches for coupe and sedan, 219.3 inches for the wagon. It weighed 3,850 and 3,925 pounds for coupe and sedan, 4,000 for wagon.

The engine repertory was the 231 V-6 at 105 horsepower, rated by EPA at 16 MPG. The old in-line six, 250 CID, at the same horsepower, had 17 MPG attached to it. Then came the parade of V-8 engines, some of them offered only for certain years. The longest playing engines were the 350 V-8 (15 MPG) and the same engine with a four-barrel carburetor, which upped the horsepower and slightly decreased the mileage. But you will also find three or four other GM V-8 engines. Remember, in looking at any '70s GM product, the 350 V-8 was the workhorse. When you put a bigger carburetor on it, you could add 20 to 40 horses, but those two extra carburetor barrels didn't run on water. Prices:

Year	Prices
1975	$1,300–$2,000
1976	$2,000–$2,700
1977	$2,400–$3,400

In 1978 Cutlass was "down-sized." Now its wheelbase was 108.1 inches across the board. Its length 197.7 inches in all models. Its weight went from about 3,075 to 3,250. Engine choice was narrowed to emphasize smaller V-8s, but you could also get the V-6 and the 350 V-8.

The Cutlass Supreme added luxury and slightly different cosmetics to the basic Cutlass. So, expect it to cost a few more dollars. It's the same basic car.

Oldsmobile Delta 88 is close to Buick LeSabre. On a wheelbase of 123.5 inches, a length of 220.2, with body weight of 4,250 to 4,350, the car was and is a big guzzler. Its mid-'70s career was interrupted along with the rest of the world's vehicles by the gas crunch, and its girth came tumbling down—slightly. Prices:

Year	Prices
1975	$1,000–$2,000
1976	$1,500–$2,200

The Olds Delta 88 change in 1977 matched LeSabre, dimension for dimension, with variations in price here and there. Prices:

Year	Prices
1977	$2,300–$3,500
1978	$2,800–$4,100
1979	$3,600–$5,200
1980	$4,500–$6,300
1981	$7,655–$8,678

Oldsmobile 98 is a close relative of Buick Electra and Cadillac DeVille. Its 1975–76 figures show a wheelbase of 127 inches, a length of 226.1, a weight of 4,700, 4,800, and 5,000—two-door, four-door, and wagon, respectively.

Engines were the 400- and 455-CID V-8s. These cars couldn't pass a gas station, though EPA rated them at 11 to 13.5 MPG. Prices:

Year	Prices
1975	$1,100–$1,900
1976	$1,700–$2,650

The "down-sized" Olds 98 follows Buick Electra and Cadillac DeVille and Fleetwood into a 118.9-inch wheelbase, a 220.4-inch length, and several smaller engines, all V-8s beginning with the 260 CID. Prices:

Year	Prices
1977	$ 2,700–$ 4,050
1978	$ 3,725–$ 5,250
1979	$ 4,700–$ 6,700
1980	$ 6,400–$ 8,825
1981	$10,778–$10,896

Oldsmobile Omega is a twin of the Chevrolet Nova–Buick Apollo. Its specifications and prices are similar. Omega, today, is the X-body Olds, identical with Citation, and so forth.

Oldsmobile Starfire is the Olds version of Monza, and its specifications and prices parallel Monza. It is best bought with the Pontiac engine, the in-line four-cylinder, nicknamed the "iron duke," the GM workhorse four.

Olds Toronado, like Cadillac Eldorado, was a front-drive "personal luxury" behemoth through most of the '70s. On a wheelbase of 122.3 inches, a length of 222, and a weight of about 5,300 pounds, it used the 403- and 455-CID engines, the latter with 350 horsepower. Prices:

Year	Prices
1975	$1,100–$2,000
1976	$1,600–$2,500
1977	$2,700–$4,150
1978	$3,650–$5,000

In 1979 Toronado shrunk to a 113.9-inch wheelbase, a length of 205.6 inches, and a weight of about 4,000 pounds. Engines were the 307 and 350 V-8s. Mileages picked up to EPA numbers of 15 and with the fuel-injected 350 V-8 to 24 MPG.

The car continues to resemble the new Eldorado, but prices are different.

Year	Prices
1979	$ 6,500–$8,250
1980	$ 8,000–$9,975
1981	$12,526

Pontiac Astre is the same as the Vega, except that it dispensed with the Vega engine in 1977 for the "iron-duke" new GM four-cylinder. Prices:

Year	Prices
1975	$ 800–$1,750
1976	$1,300–$2,100
1977	$1,600–$2,325

Incidentally, there were fewer complaints about rust with Astre; there were also fewer sold.

Pontiac Bonneville/Catalina was Pontiac's land yacht of the early and mid-1970s. If at all possible, it is best avoided. This goes for all the oversized hulks, but not the intermediates and those cars you find in good condition, no matter what their age and size. So, Bonneville/Catalina could fit into our category of good used cars for the money, if the usual ifs are satisfied.

In 1975 the car had a wheelbase of 123.5, a length of 226, a weight of between 4,500 and 5,000. Engines were all the V-8 biggies by GM—two 350 combinations, two 400, and one 455 CID. *Combinations* refers to engine-carburetor teams, with a four-barrel delivering more horsepower and less mileage. Mileages were 11 to 13.5. Prices:

Year	Prices
1975	$ 900–$2,000
1976	$1,400–$2,400

The 1977 Bonneville/Catalina now resembles the Buick LeSabre, Olds Delta 88, and Chevy Caprice/Impala. Prices:

Year	Prices
1977	$2,200–$3,600
1978	$2,800–$4,700
1979	$3,400–$5,650
1980	$4,400–$6,975
1981	$7,543–$9,381

Pontiac Firebird is a cult car, with some interest to collectors. The car remained more or less frozen in its pony car mold throughout the '70s, a mold it inherited from the '60s. Firebird appears to be immortal, like the Stravinsky ballet suite. It is also a twin of Camaro, which has most, but not all, of the same engine selection. So, if you can't find what you want in one car, you can find it in the other. They have different grilles and

FIGURE 51. The Chevy Camaro. Along with the Pontiac Firebird, it became a cult car; they are more alike than not.

back-end cosmetics, but they are otherwise identical. They each have a big, dedicated following. So good.

Firebird and Camaro have always been charming cars to drive, observe and maintain. However, if you look at an early- or mid-'70s example, beware of the two-speed automatic transmission and rust.

On a wheelbase of 108.2, length 198.1, and weight of 3,400 pounds, the cars had the two GM six-cylinder engines, and every V-8 in the book. The 350 is all you need and is best for mileage. Prices:

Year	Prices
1975	$ 1,600–$2,500
1976	$ 2,200–$3,125
1977	$ 2,500–$3,800
1978	$ 3,300–$4,800
1979	$ 4,000–$5,700
1980	$ 4,800–$7,100
1981	$12,257

These prices are official list, but are to be taken with a grain of salt. Firebird is already becoming a collector's item and it is likely to get more expensive than blue book prices suggest. Recent models, of course, don't interest collectors.

Pontiac Grand Prix is Monte Carlo in Pontiac clothing. It is the same as that car, but plenty of people will deny it heatedly because the cosmetics and interiors are different enough to set them apart. Also, they do have slightly different road feel if you compare suspension treatments. Prices are somewhat but not much different. Prices:

Year	Prices
1975	$1,400–$2,200
1976	$1,800–$2,700
1977	$2,600–$3,500

Grand Prix in 1978 had the GM shrink applied to it. It's now on the 108.1-inch wheelbase—that popular number. Prices:

Year	Prices
1978	$3,300–$4,500
1979	$3,900–$5,200
1980	$4,700–$6,300
1981	$7,614–$9,197

If a "personal luxury" car is your bag, it is difficult to find a better one than these coupes. They were marvelous cars when they came out; they remain excellent if you get the right one. They don't have much space for passengers or luggage, but they have an opulent interior for two people.

Pontiac LeMans is a GM standard, with Chevelle and all the intermediates, especially Skylark and Cutlass. They are clones, great cars, durable, desirable—and guzzlers in the mid 1970s. They weren't perceived that way in their heyday. On the contrary, they were considered an interesting balance between luxury and economy. In the context of their times, they were. But now their economy has vanished, and unless you get the right car, you may have difficulty identifying their luxury, in view of what has developed in recent years in that field.

In place of the concert hall stereo realism modern cars beam at you, complete with tape devices, these cars had squeaky little monophonic radios without cassettes. Nevertheless, they were great cars, hard to fault and good buys today.

LeMans, in 1975 and 1976, was on a wheelbase of 112 and 116 (two-door and four-door). Their lengths were 207.4 and 211.4, their weights were 3,625, 4,000, and—for the station wagon—4,300. Prices:

Year	Prices
1975	$1,100–$2,600
1976	$1,800–$2,900
1977	$2,100–$3,250

The new versions, in 1978, have the crowded number, 108.1 inches for wheelbase. Fuel economy is better, as with the other cars of this size. Prices:

Year	Prices
1978	$2,800–$4,100
1979	$3,500–$5,000
1980	$4,300–$6,000
1981	$6,856–$7,893

Pontiac Phoenix is the GM X-body, front-drive car, with the same specifications as the others (Citation, and so on). Prices:

Year	Prices
1980	$4,700–$6,300
1981	$6,307–$6,969

Pontiac Sunbird is the racier version of Vega/Astre and a clone of Monza. The first engines in 1976 were the Vega four-cylinder, later the V-6, V-8, and the in-line "iron duke" four. Prices:

Year	Prices
1976	$2,000–$2,700
1977	$2,300–$3,100
1978	$2,900–$4,000
1979	$3,300–$4,400
1980	$4,200–$5,300

Pontiac Ventura merged with Phoenix in 1975, for a run at the 111-inch wheelbase market. It butted heads with Skylark and Omega in the '75-to-'79 vintages. Ventura's engines started with the "iron duke" four cylinder and went up to the four-barrel 350 V-8. Prices:

Year	Prices
1975	$1,300–$2,100
1976	$1,800–$2,700
1977	$2,300–$3,500
1978	$2,800–$4,100
1979	$3,200–$4,700

Phoenix became the X-body Pontiac, identical with the others, as we have noted.

15

Foreign Car Prices

AUDI

Audi Fox is similar enough to VW Dasher, which is similar enough to VW Rabbit, to be discussed with those cars. Wheelbase is 97.2 inches, length 172 inches, weight 2,000 to 2,300. Prices:

Year	Prices
1975	$1,500–$2,400
1976	$1,900–$3,100
1977	$2,400–$3,625
1978	$3,100–$4,575

Audi 4000 succeeded the Fox in 1979. The same power train basics are here, but with many new systems, including fuel injection not present in the first Rabbits. Dimensions are slightly different, though there are many similarities. However, the 1980 4000 offers the five-cylinder engine.

FIGURE 52. VW Rabbit dominated European front-drive design and much of similar U.S. lines—by Chrysler, especially.

Wheelbase is 99.8, length is 176.6, weight is 2,146 to 2,537 pounds. Rear leg room is much improved, from the earlier inadequate 29 inches (two-door) and 31 inches (four-door) to 33.5 inches in both models. Prices:

Year	Prices
1979	$6,000–$7,700
1980	$7,950–$9,750

Audi 4000 became 5-plus-5 for 1981. It has been upgraded in various particulars, to become a luxury, medium-sized car. With the five-cylinder engine, it also has a five-speed over-drive, stick shift. Mileage with this engine is rated at 21 MPG. Its 1981 price is $11,105, new.

Audi's 100LS, which was supposed to rival the BMW through the 1970s, did not enhance Germany's reputation for trouble-free engines. It had electronic fuel injection and was a very smooth performing car, but it aroused a lot of complaints about service, perhaps many of them because of the novelty of the high prices generally imposed by imports. As we stress, electronic fuel injection is a chancy system.

On a wheelbase of 105.3 inches, length of 187.2 inches, weighing 2,570 pounds, the car had only the usual Audi (Rabbit) engine, but with fuel injection in the 1975-to-1977 models.

As a front-drive luxury sedan, you could do a lot worse at the right price. Prices:

Year	Prices
1975	$1,600–$2,375
1976	$2,200–$3,125
1977	$2,750–$3,775

Though we recommend not buying any used car earlier than 1975, you could make out a good case for earlier Audis, since they didn't change that much. If you find a 1974 or even a '73 in the pink and can get it at a respectable price, it could be an excellent car.

Audi 5000 replaced the 100LS in 1978. Its wheelbase at 105.5, length of 188.9, and other specifications make it slightly larger and roomier, with a generous rear leg room of 37 inches. Engines are the five-cylinder with fuel injection and the diesel, also five-cylinder. Mileages are from 17 to 30 (diesel) MPG.

This luxury sedan will appeal to people who would like to own a BMW but can't afford it. The Audi has very high quality engineering designs and specifications, and the five-cylinder engine has demonstrated that it can go the same distance as a six or eight. The similarities with Rabbit should not obscure the advances and differences in this car. Any used Audi is of interest, but this one is even more so. Prices:

Year	Prices
1978	$ 5,300–$ 6,825
1979	$ 6,400–$ 8,100
1980	$ 8,400–$10,200

1981 $11,240–$17,650
1981 (Diesel) $12,090–$13,690

The Audi 5000 Turbo is one further step up the Audi line. This luxury sports sedan is identical with the 5000 just described, except that the turbocharger adds dollars. Price: 1981, $17,650.

BMW

BMW is a small luxury sedan that projects sports car imagery in its promotion. It has quasi–cult status, certainly in its recent past, that could translate into investment status in the future. An advertising promotion suggests that it could be better than stocks and bonds. However, bull markets in cars take decades to get going; in equities they can start anytime.

BMW is terribly expensive and costly to maintain and repair, and it isn't that much better to drive than cars costing about half its current price ranges. That is true of virtually every expensive car and is not mentioned here to detract from BMW, which is an excellent car, with an interesting power train, suspension, body, and cosmetics.

Until 1976 the 2002 was about the only BMW in the U.S. Between 1973 and 1976 it was priced between $2,000 and $5,200. Beware of the early models, especially for rust, and if major transmission and engine work are needed (they almost certainly will be if the car has heavy mileage), the prices will be astronomical, mostly for parts and labor. The 2002 was an interesting car in many ways. It offered an overhead cam, four-cylinder engine, good gas mileages with fuel injection—which it had when nobody in the U.S. had every heard of it—and an interesting suspension system.

BMW 320i replaced 2002 as the smaller car in the line on a wheelbase of 100.9 inches. Slightly longer, at 177.5, and heavier, 2,650 pounds, and less sparing of gas, it used the same engine. Anyone used to power steering will not like this car at parking time. Anyone used to buying low-priced cars won't like it at buying time. Prices:

Year	Prices
1977	$ 5,600–$ 7,200
1978	$ 6,525–$ 8,200
1979	$ 7,600–$ 9,975
1980	$ 9,500–$11,750
1981	$12,895

BMW medium-sized models include 530i and the similar 528i. These cars are on a wheelbase of 103.8 inches, with a length of 190 at 3,325 pounds, and with a fuel-injected, overhead cam, six-cylinder engine rated at 169 horsepower in the 1979–81 models. A slightly more powerful version of the same engine is found in the 1975–78 models. Both get about 19 MPG on the EPA rating. Prices:

Year	Prices
1975	$ 5,000–$ 6,400
1976	$ 5,850–$ 7,300
1977	$ 6,700–$ 8,400
1978	$ 8,700–$11,200
1979	$11,000–$13,700
1980	$14,000–$19,500
1981	$15,300–$22,000

DATSUN

Datsun, which becomes Nissan in the U.S. as well as in Japan, has flooded the U.S. markets with a variety of models, as has Toyota, its rival here and everywhere else.

Datsun's B-210 has been prowling our streets for years. It has only two things going for it: mileage and price. It's a tacky car, poor to ride, drive, accelerate, poor in comfort and convenience. Though no recalls are charged against it, the car rusted, had electrical and other standard problems, and repair prices were and remain high.

The car in the 1975–78 models is on a wheelbase of 92.1

inches, a length of 163 inches, a weight of about 2,000 pounds. Engines are the overhead cam, four-cylinder, 85 CID rated at 83 horsepower. Miles per gallon is among the best; 28.1. Prices:

Year	Prices
1975	$1,200–$2,025
1976	$1,500–$2,475
1977	$1,850–$3,200
1978	$2,300–$3,850

In 1979 the 210 was changed for the better. Riding comfort improved a bit, but the car remained about what it was: something to get you from here to there, and to get you little else other than economy. That seems to be enough. Dimensions are basically the same, with an engine that is now rated at 91 CID, giving the car better acceleration and, amazingly enough, better mileage. The car is now rated at 27.4 to 35 MPG. Prices:

Year	Prices
1979	$2,800–$4,200
1980	$3,300–$4,875

Datsun F-10, a 1976-to-1978 entrant, is front drive. In most other ways it's the B-210. It seems to have assumed the worst aspects of both front- and rear-drive small cars: uncomfortable riding qualities, steering, seating, visibility, and stability. Again, no recall notices.

Dimensions are a 94.3-inch wheelbase, 170.1-inch length, 2,368 pounds in weight, with the Datsun overhead cam four-cylinder, 119 CID rated at 92 horsepower and 23.2 miles per gallon. Prices:

Year	Prices
1977	$2,600–$3,525
1978	$3,200–$4,150
1979	$3,800–$4,875

Datsun 200-SX is a sports coupe version of the B-210. Its numbers are similar to that car, though its weight is 2,360. Engine is the peppier 119-CID four-cylinder with 92 horses and 23.2 MPG. Prices:

Year	Prices
1977	$2,600–$3,525
1978	$3,200–$4,150
1979	$3,800–$4,875

FIGURE 53. A Datsun 200-SX hatchback SL from 1980. This car is the sports version of the 510; prior to 1980 it was based on the 210. So buy the 1980, all else being equal.

The 200-SX 1980 is based on the 510 line rather than the 210, so it's a better car. It represents Datsun at its best, which is very good indeed. On a wheelbase of 94.5 inches, length 176.4 inches, weight of 2,635 pounds, with the 119-CID engine rated at 100 horses. EPA mileage is 25. Prices:

Year	Prices
1980	$4,200–$5,300
1981	$7,189–$8,489

Datsun 310 is a front-drive, updated version of the F-10, with improvements but not enough to compete with other American and Japanese small cars, especially Honda Civic.

On a 94.3-inch wheelbase with 160.6 inches in length, weight of 2,000, 85-CID engine of 65 horses and 30 MPG, the car has these prices:

Year	Prices
1979	$3,100–$4,200
1980	$3,700–$4,900
1981	$5,339–$6,239

Datsun 510, starting in 1978, is an old-style, rear-drive car, aimed at economy, durability, and family outings, which the Japanese imagine Americans remember longingly because cars like that used to exist. It's about like a '51 Chevrolet, allowing for such modernities as emission control and the engine modifications involved.

Wheelbase is 94.5, length 169.9, weight 2,265, the engine 119 CID rated at 28 MPG. Prices:

Year	Prices
1978	$2,800–$4,075
1979	$3,300–$4,600
1980	$3,800–$5,100
1981	$6,189–$6,889

Datsun 610, between 1973 and 1976, is similar enough to 710, 1974–77, to be discussed together. Both cars use the 108- and 119-CID four-cylinder engines, with mileages around 22 MPG. Other numbers are fairly similar, with the 610 heavier and longer, more sluggish. Neither car is famous for sprightliness. The heavier one would be even less peppy.

Wheelbases are 98.4 and 96.5; lengths are 174.8 and 169.3. Weights are 2,633 and 2,323. Prices:

Year	Prices
1975	$1,500–$2,400
1976	$1,900–$2,800
1977	$2,200–$3,300

Datsun "Z" cars are the Japanese Corvette. They are gadget-prone, eye-catching, sex object cars, lusted after by males and females alike. As with other sports cars, they are impractical, a fact that merely emphasizes their endearments. They also ride like small trucks, another characteristic that makes them irresistible to their fans, most of whom wouldn't be caught dead driving a truck.

Recent models have electronic fuel injection systems, manual or automatic transmission, a four-wheel strut suspension system, with universal joints at the rear wheels for independent movements, four-wheel disk brakes, an overhead cam, in-line, six-cylinder engine, rated at 180 horsepower. The car weighs about 3,000 pounds. The 280 ZX has turbocharging, to make it the most powerful thing on the road, at least in short spurts (that's the turbocharger). This car even has power windows. 1981 prices range from $11,300 to $17,000.

Early "Z" cars kept their prices high. Few are around, and any of them in good condition would be expensive, no matter what year. A 1975 "Z" would sell for at least $2,500, and a lot more if in good shape.

Datsun 810, between 1977 and 1980 was a 104.3-inch wheelbase car, 183.5 inches in length, weighing 2,756 pounds, with overhead cam, six-cylinder engine rated at 118 horse-power at 19 MPG. Fuel injection, in 1980, raised both the horsepower (120) and mileage (21). The car was redesigned in 1981, using the same engine, however. It is more luxurious, more expensive, but not much better. It's on a 103.5-inch wheelbase, length of 183.3 inches, weight of 2,800 pounds. Prices:

Year	Prices
1977	$2,700–$ 3,825
1978	$3,500–$ 4,550
1979	$4,200–$ 5,325
1980	$4,900–$ 6,000
1981	$7,979–$10,879

FIAT

Fiat 131 and Brava are rear-drive, conventional 98-inch wheel-base cars. Fiat's length is 172.4 inches, weight 2,450 pounds, its engine is an overhead cam, four-cylinder rated at about 86 horsepower with about 21 MPG. Complaints about the car involve mostly the high cost of parts and repairs, rust damage, and premature breakdown of some systems—not exactly novel complaints. Prices:

Year	Prices
1975	$1,200–$2,125
1976	$1,600–$2,600
1977	$1,900–$3,100
1978	$3,000–$4,500
1979	$3,400–$4,900
1980	$4,000–$5,400
1981	$8,190–$8,390

Fiat Strada is a front-drive car on a 96.4-inch wheelbase, 161 inches in length, weighing 2,100. Its overhead cam four-cylinder engine is a 91-CID with excellent mileage: 29 MPG.

This is the car that has given Fiat the best image in the U.S. It's a great little subcompact front drive, competitive with the best of them, including VW, Omni, and so on. Prices:

Year	Prices
1979	$3,000–$4,200
1980	$3,600–$5,100
1981	$4,689–$6,357

Fiat Spider is a cult sportster, not unlike the TR7 convertible. It's a two-seater, front engine, rear drive, with a double-overhead cam engine, lately with fuel injection. Wheelbase is 89.7 inches, length 163, weight 2,360 pounds, mileage about 25.

FIGURE 54. Fiat Spider is a front-engine sports car in contrast to the X1/9 mid-engine car.

Prices on the Spider depend on what the traffic will bear, condition, and mileage, but the 1981 with standard equipment lists for about $9,900. Earlier models would subtract about $1,000 for a one-year-old, $1,500 for a two-year-old, and so on. Few of them exist in the U.S.; they are highly sought after, so list prices don't mean much. Young people adore them.

Fiat X1/9, with an engine midway in this tiny sports car,

is another cult car by Fiat, also few in number in the U.S. and more experimental than the Spider. It's quite an amazing car and considering the price is also quite a bargain, if that's the right word. Bargain implies something necessary or essential; this is all frivolity and charm, masquerading as transportation.

The car is a two-door coupe on a wheelbase of 86.7 inches, with length of 156.2 inches, weight of 2,130 pounds. Its overhead cam engine is rated at 26 to 30 MPG, with fuel injection accounting for the higher mileage. The engine itself is similar to the one used in the current Strada.

The price situation is similar to Spider. In 1981 the car listed for $8,997; earlier models decrease like the progression indicated for Spider, with the same "whatever the traffic will bear" situation in force.

HONDA

Honda Accord made an enormous impact when it arrived in 1976. It was scarce and had a reputation for working miracles with a gallon of gas, based on the performance of Honda Civic, which preceded it in 1973. It made a big splash because of its luxury qualities, missing on most Japanese cars, and because it had an innovative engine and front-drive power transmission, which was coveted in those days and scarce. Honda's engine is a stratified charge in which an extra combustion process occurs inside a mini-chamber. Fuel thus burns more completely, with lower emissions. But the engine can be balky in hot starts in some models, so you do well to try it out. Honda takes a lot of expensive maintenance along with saving a lot of expensive gas. It drives, rides, and handles especially well, comparing with Rabbit, Omni, and the best in the West, at least in recent models (but not early ones). Accord does not do nearly as well on gas as its smaller brother, Civic.

Accord has a wheelbase of 93.7 inches, length of 162.8, weight of 2,024 pounds. It has an overhead cam engine of advanced design, with an EPA fuel rating of about 30. The 1976 and 1977 Accords were sluggish and underpowered, compared with the later ones. Prices:

Year	Prices
1976	$2,500–$3,400
1977	$3,100–$4,150
1978	$3,600–$5,100
1979	$4,100–$6,000
1980	$4,600–$6,650
1981	$6,999–$8,049

Honda Prelude is a sporty version of Accord, based on the Civic, and it is more expensive than Accord and Civic.

Honda Civic was the Japanese front-drive, transverse engine calling card in the U.S. The stratified charge engine (CVCC) was avant-garde machinery in 1973, and it still is. The U.S. doesn't make one. The funny-looking car quickly melted any reservations about its size and appearance when gas mileage figures were posted just about the time of the highest OPEC hysteria. When people drove it, they were astonished at front-drive, small-car characteristics. Though Civic remains a good selling car, at the same time as it is the gas mileage champ, it has taken a redesign to make it competitive in appearance and ride with other cars of its size and design. This happened in 1980.

The car has a wheelbase of 86.6, a length of 146.9, and weight of 1,630 (possibly the lightest car in the U.S.). The engine is the standard Honda overhead cam, in three available power output capabilities: In 1973 the engine had 50 horsepower; in 1974 to 1979 it had 52 to 59, and in 1975 to 1979 a 64-horsepower engine was offered. Gas mileages were actually best in the 64-horsepower engine, thanks to a special carburetor. EPA ratings for the three engines were 25.9, about 26.5 and about 29.

The 1980 Honda Civic is on the same wheelbase, but the car is 148 inches long and weighs 1,832 pounds. Two engine capabilities are offered, the 58 and 67 horsepower, both rated at 28 MPG. Prices:

Year	Prices
1980	$3,400–$5,325
1981(two-door)	$4,599–$5,999
1981(four-door)	$4,499–$6,499

MAZDA

Mazda made a big splash with its rotary engine in the early '70s. However, the rotary engine developed terminal oil seal problems early in the game, and for all its pizzazz and power, got only mediocre gas mileage. A small, high-performance engine, the rotary was improved in later models, but the early oil seal disasters had colored public thinking, and the car's sales dropped off to a tiny percentage.

Today's Mazda rotary engines are far better. In fact, the engine is one of the most reliable in the business. Both the early models, RX-2 and RX-3, cannot be recommended. Their careers, respectively, were from 1971 to 1975, and from 1972 to 1978. Anyone interested in them, and willing to take the risk and the gas-buying expense, can buy them for a song. RX-4, (1974 to 1978), though similar, had improvements, but it is still a rotary with too many burdens to bear.

Three cars by Mazda are of interest: the GLC, the 626, and the RX-7.

GLC ("Great Little Car") is a gas miser, thanks to its standard four-cylinder engine with overhead cam. For 1977 and 1978 the engine is a 78 CID rated at 64 horsepower with 31.1 MPG performance. Another version of the engine, introduced in 1979, has 83 horses from an 86-CID engine. This one gets 28.5 MPG. The car is strictly a price-mileage proposition, like Datsun 210, and competes in that market. It will not be mistaken for a classy car in any way, shape, or form.

On a wheelbase of 91.1 inches, length of 154.3, and weight of 1,965, the car is notable for a lack of rear leg room in all three models: a three-door sedan, five-door sedan, and five-door wagon. Prices:

Year	Prices
1977	$1,700–$2,650
1978	$2,200–$3,100
1979	$2,700–$3,750
1980	$3,225–$4,300
1981 (two-door)	$4,895–$6,095
1981 (four-door)	$5,895–$6,345

Mazda 626 is an excellent family-type rear-drive car, far superior to many of its rivals by Datsun and Toyota. When you look at the numbers, they aren't impressive. When you look at the car, you get another picture entirely. First the numbers: A wheelbase of 98.8, length of 173.8, weight of 2,500, an engine of 75 horsepower, 120 CID, rated at 24.5 MPG. It's a smooth performer, conventional in every way, comparable with the Datsun 610, but classier than that car. Prices:

Year	Prices
1979	$3,825–$5,000
1980	$4,400–$5,950
1981	$7,095–$8,195

Mazda RX-7 is the chief Japanese competitor to the Datsun 280-Z. It has a new rotary engine that is reputed to have overcome the oil-seal problems that plagued the earlier versions. It has their power and performance with somewhat better gas mileage. Rotary engines are a new driving experience for anyone innocent of their habits. Despite the elliptical shape of the engine block, they run more smoothly and generate far more power in a confined space of similar size than do other engines. Their maintenance is similar if they hold up. Mazda says they do, and statistics on the new rotary tend to support that contention. But remember, a typical Detroit V-8 (and probably V-6) engine will run on for 100,000 to 200,000 miles without major rebuilding incidents. Mazda rotaries have yet to prove they can equal those numbers. Four-cylinder engines may be comparable in durability with the rotary, in which case a lowering of sights may prove satisfactory, down to 75,000 to 100,000, perhaps. Let us guess that the new rotary has durability equal to most new four-cylinder engines. In that case, it far outperforms the competition, except in gas mileage, where it lags. So those are the trade-offs. Remember that General Motors spent many millions trying to develop a rotary that would compete. GM gave it up as a bad job. Contrary opinion might suggest rushing out and buying the rotary, as we've already suggested, but in this case that opinion becomes questionable. What has this to do with the Mazda RX-7? Some observers claim it is the best buy in the sports car world, viewing it solely in new-car terms. Viewing it in used-car terms puts it in a slightly different light.

FIGURE 55. The Mazda RX-7. Its rotary engine makes for a high-performance car.

When you buy a Corvette, Fiat, MGB (discontinued after 1980), a Datsun "Z" car, or any of the others, you buy a tried-and-true engine. Not so with Mazda. It is tried, but the truth of it is not so well established. Should it be viewed as a "turn-around situation," as with a stock that might regain huge losses? Anything can turn around, especially a sports car in a tight situation, but why risk it? A stock can make huge gains when it turns around, but a sports car? For a used low-priced car, the several Fiats, TR-7, or MGB would be best bets. More expensive, more exotic, would be the Datsun "Z" cars, Porsche, and Corvette (it isn't exotic meaning foreign, but exotic meaning "out of this world" in reference to unusual gadgetry and performance).

Mazda RX-7 is on a wheelbase of 95.3 inches, length of 170.1 inches, weight of 2,345 pounds. EPA rating is 21 MPG, city driving, much higher in country.

Note that the engine is a two-rotor Wankel; early ones had one rotor. 1981 prices range from $9,395 to $11,395. That's the latest new-car price. Earlier used cars, starting in 1978, could be lower, depending on the usual variables, or higher than comparable sports cars—condition, mileage, availability (the cars are very scarce).

MERCEDES-BENZ

Mercedez-Benz is the austere, formidable German sedan that has the reputation for being perfect. It is nothing of the sort, though it has had virtually no recall history. To be officially designated as "without blemish" is like being called a person of every virtue; you could also possess every vice. Mercedes doesn't have every vice or even every virtue, for that matter, though it has important numbers of each. As to vice, it is far too expensive for what you get—a smallish car with a rather stiff ride; intolerably expensive to maintain, buy parts for, and/or have repaired; and with no lack of breakdowns in the usual systems. Its virtues are so well advertised that it is hard to separate fact from fancy. It is indeed well put together and designed to stay together, within state-of-the-art limitations (its power train wears out, like every other, its body rusts, and so on). One thing it has, along with BMW, Rolls, Porsche, and a few others, is resistance to low prices. Mercedes starts life with a silver spoon in its price tag and keeps it there throughout its career. If there is a used-car heaven, Mercedes undoubtedly has price of place along with pride.

Without power steering Mercedes is stiff and awkward. Its ride is otherwise not the heavily cushioned coddle of expensive U.S. cars, but it is comfortable. Everything about the car is comfortable, bourgeois, well meaning.

FIGURE 56. A Mercedes-Benz sports coupe.

The 1975–76 Mercedes cars were on a wheelbase of 108.3 inches, a length of 195.5 inches, a weight of 3,500 pounds, with a repertory of several engines to drive the moderately heavy car. Note that the car is intermediate in weight and compact in size (barely enough rear leg room). One 1975–76 engine is the four-cylinder 141-CID rated at 93 horses, with a 26-MPG EPA ticket. The twin overhead cam, six-cylinder, with four-barrel carburetor, for 1971 to 1976, cuts gas mileage to 17.5 MPG but increases acceleration. That engine is a lulu, as slang has it: very powerful (between 120 and 157 horses), quiet, and performance oriented, like the Detroit guzzlers of old. It is a sports car engine.

Price ranges of the 1971-to-1974 Mercedes may be noted briefly as $2,800 to $6,875 (with engines and other components similar to the numbers just mentioned, with car identifications of 220, 230, 280, 280C, and the diesels with D in their numbers). One can expect to pay almost $7,000 for a 1974 car that could post several hundred thousand miles on it. The advantage is clearly to the seller, so avoid such cars as you would the plague if you are a rational used-car buyer.

Prices for 1975–76 models just discussed:

Year	Prices
1975	$5,000–$7,900
1976	$5,800–$9,500

These cars are priced as if they were immortal. They are not.

In 1977 Mercedes offered a new small car with the usual choice of gasoline or diesel engines. Mercedes is a pioneer in diesel technology, and its engines have a superlative record of long, efficient performance. If you love a diesel—that is, you are a closet trucker—you cannot find a diesel to equal Mercedes in durability and reliability. You can find plushier ones at General Motors, and they also cost a lot less and are more likely to require major repair and maintenance work. However, anything you do to a General Motors car costs less than almost everything you do or have done to a Mercedes. I do not refer to windshield wiper blade replacement, spark plugs, and so on, which tend to cost the same the world over, or even when they cost more, the dollars don't amount to much. I refer to the breakdown systems. It is not generally breathed about that a Mercedes transmission can conk out, like a merely mortal GM transmission, but when it does, it will cost a leg and arm to repair it, whereas the GM will cost in some cases, a signature on a guarantee, and, in other cases, two or three hundred dollars or double that if you take it to the wrong place. It will still be less than the Mercedes.

The wheelbase of the 1977 car is 106.7 inches, length is 187.5 inches, weight 3,450. Engines are the four-cylinder 141-CID rated at 19.5 MPG and 86 horsepower, and the six-cylinder fuel injected 167-CID, noted previously in the earlier car, with twin overhead cams. This one gets 17 MPG. Also available are two diesels; the four-cylinder and five-cylinder. With the four-cylinders you get 28 MPG and 3 less with the five-cylinder. Prices:

Year	Prices
1977	$ 7,200–$12,100
1978	$ 8,800–$16,000

1979	$12,000–$20,000
1980	$15,000–$26,000
1981	$26,640–$29,231

Prices such as these give you a peek into the ballpark you play in when you go shopping for a Mercedes. The car is not for the faint of heart or of pocketbook. It is also not for the buyer of goods; it's for the buyer of status.

SAAB

Saab 99 is a front-drive car of great distinction that once was not terribly expensive but—thanks to inflation, currency fluctuation, and other horrors—has become both distinctive and expensive. When you consider that the 1981 Saab four-door lists for between $12,700 and $15,100 and you can buy a Dodge Omni for about half that, and that they are not much different in size, you must ponder the problems of inflation and currency exchange. Without denying the excellence of Saab 99, which also has a turbocharger that is absent in most of the U.S. competition, the fact is that the difference between Saab and Aries are not all to the advantage of Saab. The Dodge Aries is on a wheelbase of 100 with length of 176; Saab is 99 inches in wheelbase, and 188 in length. Aries is 3 inches wider and seating room, front and rear, is similar. I could go on. You may object that Aries is made in Detroit by idiots and the Saab is made in Sweden by workers who love every bolt of it. But an assembly line is an assembly line is an assembly line, and all cars except Rolls Royce are made that way. The differences are in quality control and systems design. Saab has a more costly power train and cosmetic posh. It is more of a luxury car, its engines are a lot more powerful, and you won't get the mileages of less powerful cars. Also, turbocharging gives it great power surges that cars without can't produce. Saab has a gleaming enamel coat that is more distinctive than the acrylic of U.S. cars. It still costs twice as much, new. Used is something else, and that is what interests us.

On the lots, older Saabs can be found that might be bought for fairly reasonable prices, but beware of repair problems. Saab engines love to leak oil, and that may or may not signify anything, as we discussed earlier. Repairs, especially if extensive, are also expensive, as you can expect from any elite car. It is an elite car, and a great car in many special ways of riding, handling, driving, and so on. It uses interior space well. However, nobody every said Saab was troublefree, and despite the allure of its performance and appearance, a lot of things can and do go wrong with it. Fuel, cooling, brakes, and so on, have registered enough complaints to warrant your examining these systems carefully. Prices:

Year	Prices
1975	$1,600–$2,700
1976	$2,100–$3,400
1977	$3,100–$5,000
1978	$3,600–$5,500
1979	$4,300–$6,500
1980	$5,000–$7,450

The Saab 900 originated in 1979. It is turbocharged (optionally), more luxurious, slightly larger, with mediocre gas mileages, though EPA rates its 121-CID engine at 20 MPG. It has two mileages; the turbocharged 121 runs the horsepower from 115 of the engine without turbocharging to 135. Mileage drops to 17. Prices:

Year	Prices
1979	$ 4,800–$ 7,000
1980	$ 5,800–$ 8,250
1981	$10,400–$14,600

Note that these are prices without turbocharging. That model will add about $2,000.

SUBARU

Subaru is both a Japanese and American success story, after an early disaster. The first cars with that nameplate came over in the late 1960s. Basically, they were motorcycles with a roof over them. The engines and supporting systems were those of a motorcycle with adaptations for car appearance and performance. That car failed altogether. Subaru took a second look at the U.S. markets and sent over the genuine article, an advanced one at that. Beginning in about 1970, Subaru became a force in our automobile thinking. Unfortunately, Detroit ignored its simple, terrible lessons, though it had ample time to study them. I have already discussed Subaru at length in earlier contexts. Suffice to say, it is a tough competitor in the low-priced field. It is a car that took rust-proofing seriously at

FIGURE 57. Among other marvels of the front-drive Subaru are its low initial prices, high mileage, and its ability to use regular gas at 4 to 10 cents less per gallon. Its new SEEC-T engine means that it has an extra combustion process similar to stratified charge, as in the Honda.

an early age, like VW Rabbit, and unlike most U.S. cars especially in the low-priced field.

Because it is an advanced design, not many mechanics know much about it, especially in the early years, so it presents an odd paradox: it is advertised as a car for the home mechanic, but it isn't even a car for the professional, since so few know anything about it. As for the home mechanic, it is actually far more difficult than any home-grown product. That Simple Simon engine is nothing of the sort. The opposed four-cylinder engine layout has a lot of thorny designs to make life miserable for any unwary home mechanic who just rolls up his or her sleeves and gets to work. The best advice is—don't—without a lot of study. I mentioned the inboard brakes in the front of

FIGURE 58. Here's the way the Subaru SEEC-T engine works: An air suction process forces fresh air into the modified cylinder head which enables the fuel to burn more completely.

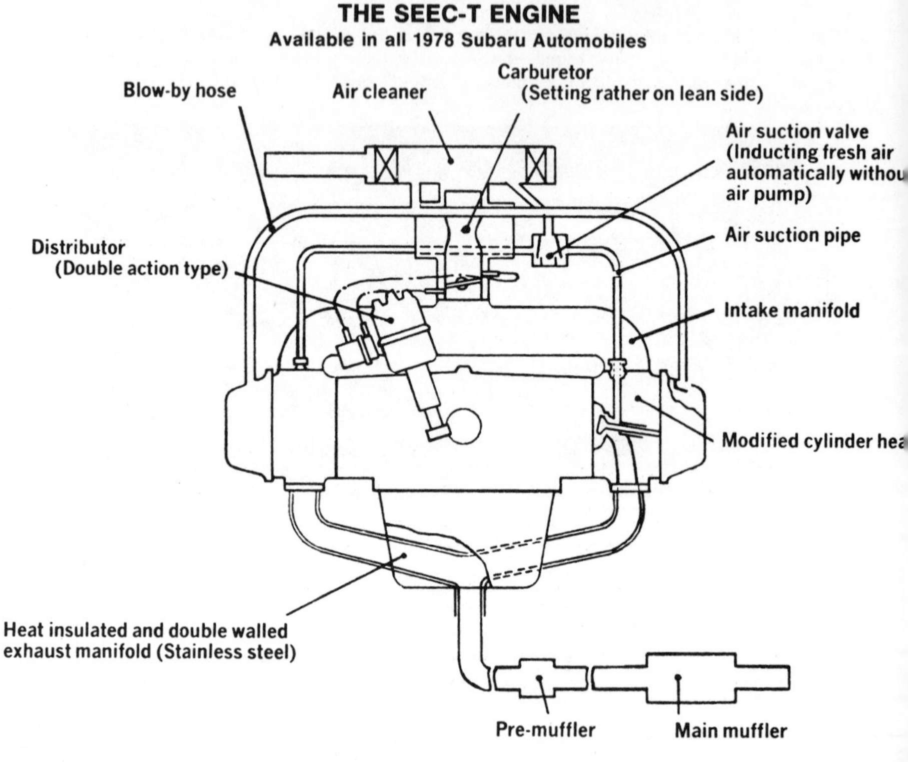

THE SEEC-T ENGINE
Available in all 1978 Subaru Automobiles

early models, lasting until about 1972. One can talk about these cars because the body integrity and rustproofing in them are so good that Subaru is one of the few cars worth looking at no matter what the age. Condition should be the chief consideration. Prices:

Year	Prices
1975	$1,200–$2,400
1976	$1,450–$2,800
1977	$1,700–$3,275
1978	$2,300–$4,200
1979	$2,800–$4,775
1980	$3,600–$5,400
1981	$5,828–$6,378

Note that the 1980 was redesigned, with the same power train but with a change of engine that adds a stratified charge concept to it.

Subaru makes the lowest-priced four-wheel-drive car in the U.S. It is the same basic car, with a slightly more powerful engine when you add automatic transmission. Add about $700 for the extra two-wheel drive.

TOYOTA

Toyota is as familiar in the U.S. as Chevrolet, which it almost replaced, thanks to the view in Detroit that Americans didn't want smaller, fuel-efficient cars. It isn't that Toyota is better than Chevrolet today, and Toyota certainly isn't better than a lot of other cars, including imports, but Toyota was here with the right goods when Chevrolet couldn't or wouldn't make them. As a result, the U.S. economy is paying through the nose, by exporting half our automobile jobs to Japan. Chevrolet is not the only villain, but it is one of the worst offenders. Today, Chevrolet makes Citation and the J-Car, both at least as good as anything comparable from Toyota, and probably better. So far Toyota's share of the market hasn't changed, but, because Toyota is muscling in on every market in the auto field, its share of the total U.S. car market may well expand. And, as Chrysler abandons the idea of the full-line automaker, and Ford may be next, Toyota steps in with an ever widening spectrum of cars.

One should look at Toyota from several points of view. It could not have existed in its present position, as the third full-line U.S. auto manufacturer, competing with GM and Ford, without OPEC. Had there been no OPEC, there would be no Toyota replacing Chrysler, which is what Toyota has done. No matter what happens in the future, Toyota has marched into the U.S. and elbowed Chrysler out. Essentially, Chrysler is reduced to two cars: Omni/Horizon and Reliant/Aries. All other cars from Chrysler-Dodge-Plymouth are variants. The fact is Reliant/Aries is Omni/Horizon in disguise, so that for all practical purposes Chrysler is now reduced to one car (as of this writing the status of Newport/New Yorker is not clear).

Toyota has any number of cars, and Datsun isn't all that far behind, so that Chrysler isn't number three, it is number five. American Motors is a minor branch of Renault; its number can't be located, though once upon a time it was number four. Toyota is building up its image in ways comparable to GM, Ford, and Chrysler in the 1950s, when advertising and image-forming carefully removed information content and used subliminal content and manipulation to make us feel about cars rather than think about them. Toyota's "Oh what a feeling" does that.

Is Toyota better than Chevrolet? In the crazy automobile world only success and survival count in the mass markets. Car buffs scorn Chevrolet *and* Toyota, except perhaps the newest Celica and the oldest Corvette. Toyota took away Chevrolet's crown as the world's biggest-selling car some years ago. Its aim in the U.S. is to take away the crown stateside as well. Is that possible? Anything is possible, especially with "sticker shock," a disease not yet contracted by Toyota but raging throughout the Chevrolet line. Thus far, Chevrolet has found no cure.

Toyota Corona, Corolla, Celica, Starlet, Tercel, and Cressida make up the current line of cars. Corona was redesigned in 1974, again in 1979.

Corolla, perhaps the best-selling single car in the world, had a 30 series that anchored Toyota as a car of high reliability in the '70s. It ended its reign in 1979, to be redesigned in 1980.

Toyota earned its reputation for high reliability, good performance, and great gas mileages along with a fair level of creature comfort, quality control in all visible aspects, and low price. An unbeatable combination, but it is equally absurd to think that Toyotas do not wear out, break down, strand you, and all the other acts of mayhem cars visit upon you. They do, and they rust out, too, just like those awful Detroit monsters, but nobody believes until it happens to them.

Consumer Reports magazine, which did much to establish Toyota and discredit Chevrolet, and so on, routinely refers to Toyota's "much better than average" predicted repair incidence. *Consumer Guide*, equally influential, blandly repeats the same formula but never examines the formula. As argued earlier, there is little reason to believe in such formulas.

Toyota is a conservative car, like Datsun, perhaps better, but does it have a car as good as Citation or Reliant, in those price ranges? Its Tercel is brand new, a good little car and competitive, probably the first of a long line. There is no doubt that Toyota can do anything it sets out to do, and if it is now determined to make first-class front-drive cars, it will certainly succeed. Tercel compares well with the competition—Citation, Omni, and so on. The clincher with Toyota is always that it can offer a price advantage. Tercel costs less than Citation or Omni. There is no reason why it shouldn't, given the wage and productivity differentials, but is it a better car? No. It has similar gas mileages but not the ridability of Citation and Omni, to say nothing of Rabbit. These basic cars are the class of their field, along with their derivatives. This field, be it noted, is *the* mass field of today and for as far into the future as the eye can see. Toyota, you can be sure, will be there in force. But so will Subaru.

Celica, from 1976 to 1977, was on a wheelbase of 98.3 inches, 174.6 inches in length, weighing 2,545, with a 134-CID overhead cam engine generating 96 horsepower. EPA rates it at 21.2 MPG. This car replaced the 1971–75 Celica by putting the slightly larger Corona engine in it and enlarging earlier numbers all around, including three lovely leg room inches in the rear seat. Important gas mileage was also added.

Then in 1978 a redesigned Celica and Supra came along, again on slightly enlarged numbers. The big difference is that a six-cylinder engine was added to the basic four-cylinder. The six, the Supra, is more luxurious, livelier, with a flashy, sporty look to it. Again it's a solid car. Celica retains most of the earlier systems. Prices:

Year	Prices
1975	$1,800–$2,674
1976	$2,200–$3,275
1977	$2,800–$4,125
1978	$3,100–$4,650
1979	$3,875–$5,200
1980	$4,600–$6,000
1981	$6,909–$8,669

Supra prices: add $1,500 to $2,500.

Corolla was on a wheelbase of 93.3 inches between 1975 and 1979. It has a length of 165.2 inches, a weight of 2,174 pounds, with rear leg room of 34.1 inches. It's the rear-drive Toyota power train, with the workhorse overhead-cam four-cylinder engine. Between 1977–1979 the output was rated at 58 horsepower, 71 CID, and mileage of 28.6. The 1977–79 higher-powered engine was 97 CID, 75 horses, 26 MPG. Prices:

Year	Prices
1975	$1,300–$2,600
1976	$1,600–$2,850
1977	$1,950–$3,500
1978	$2,600–$3,950
1979	$2,800–$4,625
1980	$3,400–$5,125
1981	$5,178–$7,588

Note that the Corolla was redesigned in 1980 with very similar numbers and mechanical systems, with a slightly more powerful engine (108 CID) that gets the same mileages. Somewhat better riding qualities, but nothing to write home about compared with our choices for that characteristic: such cars as Citation, Omni, VW, Renault 5.

Corona outsells other Toyota cars in the U.S. It's a price proposition, also it has had a long, honorable history of durability and gas economy. It will get you from here to there, not in style, but intact.

Between 1975 and 1978 Corona was on a wheelbase of 98.4 inches, with a length of 173.2 inches, a weight of 2,525 pounds, with rear leg room of 33.9 inches, with the 134-CID engine rated at 96 horsepower and 21.5 MPG. Prices:

Year	Prices
1975	$1,500–$2,600
1976	$1,800–$3,025
1977	$2,200–$3,450
1978	$2,700–$3,925

Corona's new design in 1979 was cosmetic; the power trains are the same, but with better suspension—less rocky. Prices:

Year	Prices
1979	$3,400–$4,525
1980	$4,000–$5,425
1981	$6,909–$8,669

The present Corona remains an obstinate rear-drive car, with excellent mileage, simplicity of designs where they count—in the breakdown systems—and with a fair ride and use of space. All this at a price that is no longer lower than the competition. The competition, from Detroit and elsewhere, is more advanced, utilizing front drive and hence making better use of space and offering far better traction in wet and snowy weather. Given the fact that plenty of front-drive cars are now available from all over, one can recommend Toyota only in warmer places, where traction isn't an issue. Where it is an issue, it becomes very important, and there one should go front drive. I cannot emphasize this enough. If you are determined to buy a Toyota in Boston, Chicago, or Minneapolis, buy Tercel.

Cressida is a six-cylinder Toyota with fuel injection, a plushier car with softer ride and conveniences, brought over in 1978. It's on a wheelbase of 104.9 inches, length of 184.8 inches, weighing 2,604, with a mileage rating of 21.1 in the fuel injected version, 19 with carburetor.

The car was redesigned in 1981, to add various creature comforts, safety features, and luxuries, as well as riding and performance features of some difference. Basically, the power train is the same. Prices:

Year	Prices
1978	$3,925–$ 5,125
1979	$4,600–$ 5,850
1980	$5,350–$ 6,525
1981	$11,099–$11,549

Tercel uses a standard four-cylinder Toyota engine for its front-drive power and conventional strut suspension for the transaxle connections. The engine doesn't give the car the zip other front-drives possess, but Tercel is quite a competitor in many ways. Prices:

Year	Prices
1980	$3,000–$5,625
1981	$4,548–$5,808

VOLKSWAGEN

VW Rabbit, Beetle, Dasher, and Scirocco, are all familiar names. Rabbit, Dasher, and Scirocco are variations on a single theme; the basic VW front-drive power train. Beetle is, of course, the rear-drive, rear-engine "bug."

First, the Beetle. That car goes back to Hitler, who thought of its predecessor as the "people's car." At the height of its popularity in the '50s and '60s, when it seemed invincible, the VW Beetle was selling in the hundreds of thousands, while Detroit looked on aghast. In dinosaur pace, Detroit finally reacted with the Corvair, which was supposed to brush away the tormentor (Japan had not yet made its own all-out assault on the American auto market).

Corvair, with its rear-engine, opposing pancake engine, was a masterpiece of a car. Unfortunately, it ran afoul of the U.S. consumerist movement, led by Ralph Nader, whose knowledge of cars may have been scant but whose ability at propaganda was on the order of a V-8 with fuel injection. General Motors didn't like it either, for reasons never made clear, and once the flaws in the car were removed (in about 1964) there never was a better, small car manufactured out of Detroit. Nader's contention was that you could turn the Corvair over too easily, and, yes, you *can* turn *any* car over if you are determined and foolish enough to try it.

Corvair didn't endure; the bug did, lasting in the U.S. for about thirty years. That was its trouble. VW considered it a perfect car, and perfection in cars is similar to people; just when you expect one thing based on an ideal, reality intrudes. Reality, in this case, was the automotive developments elsewhere; especially in Japan. The bug's engine was weak, the car was a fright to ride in insofar as comfort, luxury, convenience, and entertainment were concerned, and once you got past the sterling gas mileage there wasn't much else to recommend it. In a kind of Hegelian calling out of opposites, rear engine, rear drive led to front engine, front drive. (German car, German philosophy.) At the moment that looks like the higher synthesis. Of course, it could go the other way.

Maybe the car of the future will have the engine and drive train in the center, where Fiat presently locates part of it in the X1/9? Regardless, VW refused to change, and the world continues to buy the Beetle, though it is presently made outside Germany. So many small industries grew up around the world to support the Beetle that VW couldn't cut it off or expect to replace it with the totally new technology of the Rabbit without dire political and economic consequences. Nonetheless, world affection for the car wasn't turned off when the Rabbit appeared, especially after all the Rabbit's faults became known.

Between 1975 and 1979 the Beetle changed little, but fuel injection was added in 1975. Anyone buying the used car today for basic transportation should know that parts are becoming scarce and expensive, and that will get worse. However, it is a cult car, so its price could go up in the years ahead, if you have that kind of patience and space.

The wheelbase is 94.5 inches; length 158.6; weight is 1,825. The engine between 1975 and 1979 is the 97-CID with 48 horsepower. Gas mileages are figured at about 23. Prices:

Year	Prices
1975	$1,900–$2,400
1976	$2,000–$2,700
1977	$2,500–$3,500
1978	$4,200–$5,400
1979	$5,000–$6,200

Dasher came first in the new VW team of Rabbit-Dasher. It was born in 1973, a clone of Audi Fox. The Audi Fox engine isn't much different from the subsequent Rabbit. Dasher, Rabbit, and Scirocco can be considered a theme and its variations, with Rabbit the basic theme: a front-drive car that will get economy along with modern designs in all other systems, including convenience, luxury, and cosmetic appeal. Rabbit does this as well as any other car. In fact, it is better than most. Scirocco and Dasher merely add a few amenities and costs.

Dasher is on a wheelbase of 97.2 inches, with a length of 172.8 inches, weight of 2,200 pounds, rear leg room of 29 and 31 inches (two-door, four-door). Neither is adequate by American standards. Prices:

Year	Prices
1975	$1,800–$2,900
1976	$2,500–$3,600

1977	$3,200–$4,300
1978	$3,700–$5,000
1979	$4,700–$6,400
1980	$5,400–$7,100

Rabbit is on a wheelbase of 94.5 inches, length of 155 inches, weight of 2,225 pounds. The car has the same engine from 1975 on, with modifications to several systems, including the valve train in which the valve guides wear out prematurely, causing oil to burn excessively. However, fuel systems have changed; VW engineers couldn't decide whether it was more efficient to use a carburetor or fuel injectors. The question was finally resolved in favor of fuel injection, which has been used from 1976 on. Carburetors are still out there, and you have to look to see which car has it and which doesn't. Advantage? Fuel injection gets better mileage, though it cuts down on power. Prices:

Year	Prices
1975	$1,600–$ 2,400
1976	$1,900–$ 3,000
1977	$2,500–$ 4,100
1978	$3,000–$ 4,750
1979	$3,600–$ 5,800
1980	$4,000–$ 6,550
1981	$5,760–$10,505

VW Scirocco is an Italian-style version of the Rabbit. It is identical mechanically and costs more.

VOLVO

Volvo has been in this country for many years, turning from a car once famous for economy and durability to a luxury sedan. It doesn't change much. In fact, the basic Volvo four-cylinder engine is one of the oldest engines still in circulation. That testifies to its ruggedness and the obstinacy of its makers. After all, you could take any Detroit engine of the '50s or '60s and make it work in any modern car with a few additions and deletions, mostly involving emission control. Most people wouldn't know the difference, except to prefer them, until they added up the extra cost of gas.

Volvo's small engine is stingy with gas. Today, the fuel-injected four-cylinder is rated at about 20 MPG and one six-cylinder is 18 MPG (the V-6), the other in-line six is rated at up to 26 MPG.

Volvo is a hard case to classify. It is viewed as a Mercedes rival. Prices hold up well in the used-car market. The machine holds up pretty well, but not any better than most others. Its rear-drive conservatism has been offset somewhat by strut suspension, four-wheel disk brakes, and rack-and-pinion steering, which give it a modern road feel. The car is on a 104 inch wheelbase, a length of 192.6, and weighs about 3,000 pounds. Prices:

Year	Prices
1975	$2,200–$ 5,200
1976	$2,700–$ 5,700
1977	$3,100–$ 6,200
1978	$4,000–$ 7,500
1979	$5,000–$ 8,100
1980	$5,750–$ 9,000
1981	$9,315–$15,175

Note, these prices span the two-door to the four-door wagon; they don't include turbocharging—which is optional—or the diesel engine.

As to value, the Volvo has a small, elite, growing market that keeps it in business. Its buyers may know something.

CAPTIVE IMPORTS

The captive imports—so-called because GM, Chrysler, and Ford bring them over with their own names pasted over the mostly Japanese originals—include a variety of cars. Buick

Opel, which ran through 1979, was made by a company most people never heard of: Isuzu. This replaced the German-built Opel of an earlier period. The Japanese Opel sold few cars, and it is not recommended.

Dodge Colt has been a splendid Japanese car for years. It is made by Mitsubishi, and its best years have been the rear-drive 1977 to 1979, and more recently the front-drive Colt (and Plymouth Champ).

The older rear-drive Colt wasn't terribly roomy, with back-seat leg room about 31 inches, but it was durable and a springy little car. However, the best car is the front-drive, which compares especially well with Tercel, Honda Civic, Ford Fiesta, and the Escort. It is less compelling than the slightly larger cars we prefer—Citation, and so on. Its price is one of the best things about it:

Year	Prices
1978	$3,400–$4,550
1979	$3,900–$5,250
1980	$4,400–$5,600
1981	$4,988–$5,519

Mercury Capri was built in Germany before it was manufactured in Detroit. It had the Pinto engine, which will immediately kill it as far as most buyers are concerned and that's too bad because the Pinto engine is not bad. The gas tank location has nothing to do with the engine. Moreover, the Capri 98-CID engine is British. Capri's German engine is a different animal (two of them): a 122–CID four-cylinder and a 155-CID V-6. Prices:

Year	Prices
1975	$1,100–$1,850
1976	$1,674–$2,500
1977	$2,000–$3,150

Plymouth Arrow was here between 1976 and 1980. It is a Colt of the Lancer series. It was a flashy car, aimed at the young, sporty

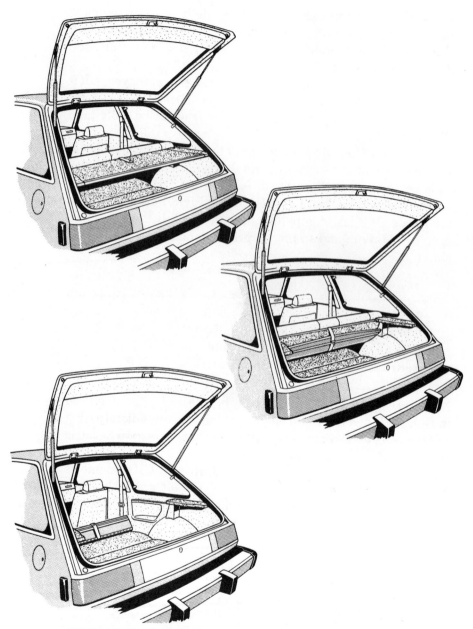

FIGURE 59. The Colt hatchback can turn itself into a quasi-station wagon by folding the back seat down and spreading out the foldaway floor.

FIGURE 60. The Plymouth Champ (top) and the Arrow (bottom) are among Chrysler's Mitsubishi connection cars.

crowd, but it didn't cut much ice with them. Prices are similar to those of the Colt.

A WORD ON IMPORTS

Since 1973 imports have been a better buy than domestic cars, and they have been essential to our industrial stability, given the OPEC assault and our inability to respond in other ways. That is changing. Finally Detroit has seen the light, but whether or not it can recover remains to be seen. At present, the issue is in doubt. Detroit is awash in red ink; it cannot sell cars profitably enough to allocate proper research and development funds. That will give Japan and Europe another competitive advantage. Ironically, the company in the worst position, Chrysler, led Detroit out of the wilderness with the Omni. However, Detroit has enough competitive product to ward off foreign competition—if only it could convince U.S. buyers that the product is, indeed, competitive. Sticker shock comes from Detroit, not Japan. As the Japanese yen regains its former strength, some advantages will tilt back to Detroit. Unless Detroit can cure sticker shock, its future is dim, even as it succeeds in curing all its other problems of labor cost, productivity, quality control, and gas mileages.

Index